DR. ELKHANAN ELKES OF THE KOVNO GHETTO

DR. ELKHANAN ELKES
OF THE
KOVNO GHETTO

A Son's Holocaust Memoir

Joel Elkes

PARACLETE PRESS
BREWSTER, MASSACHUSETTS

Library of Congress Cataloging-in-Publication Data

Elkes, Joel.
   [Values, beliefs, and survival]
   Dr. Elkhanan Elkes of the Kovno Ghetto: A Son's Holocaust
Memoir / Joel Elkes.
      p. cm.
   Originally published in Great Britain under the title: Values,
beliefs, and survival.
    Includes bibliographical references (p.   ) and index.
   ISBN 1-55725-231-9 (paperback)
    1. Jews—Persecutions—Lithuania—Kaunas. 2. Holocaust,
Jewish (1939–1945)—Lithuania—Ethnic relations. 3. Elkes,
Elkhanan, 1879–1944. 4. Kaunas (Lithuania)—Ethnic relations.
I. Title. II. Title: Doctor Elkhanan Elkes of Ghetto Kovno.
DS135.L52K3828 1999
947.93—dc21

                                         99-16657
                                             CIP

First published by Vale Publishing, London, UK, 1997.
This edition published by Paraclete Press, 1999.

10 9 8 7 6 5 4 3 2 1

© 1997, 1999 by Joel Elkes
ISBN 1-55725-231-9

Brewster, Massachusetts
www.paraclete-press.com

Printed in the United States of America.

Dedicated to my sister Sara Elkes, a quiet pioneer in intercommunity understanding who established this lecture series; and to Avraham and Pnina Tory, friends from a shared youth and intrepid messengers of light out of the great darkness.

This Memoir is based on the Inaugural Elkhanan and Miriam Elkes Memorial Lecture delivered at the Stanley Burton Center for Holocaust Studies, The University of Leicester, England, on October 31, 1991.

Contents

Foreword		ix
Preface		xiii
Acknowledgments		xv
Editor's Note		
	to the English Edition	xix
Figures		45–73
1.	Introduction	1
2.	Persons	3
3.	Carnage: The Beginning	15
4.	The Assembly	21
5.	Ghetto	25
6.	The Ninth Fort	32
7.	Work	40
8.	Joys: The Day and Beyond	78
9.	K. Z. Kauen	85
10.	The Letter	87
11.	Landsberg-Dachau	95
12.	Conversations	100
13.	Closing	109
	Notes	113
	Index	116

Foreword

The moment I met Joel Elkes, I knew I had encountered a remarkable human being. I knew nothing of his personal history, but I knew instinctively the most important thing one can know about another person: here stands someone who has suffered greatly, but in whom suffering has been transformed from bitter wound into abiding grace, deep compassion, and active, outreaching love.

Now, through this book—Joel Elkes' powerful and moving memorial to his father, Dr. Elkhanan Elkes, a physician and the courageous leader of the Kovno Ghetto in Lithuania—I have learned some of the historical facts behind Joel's suffering and that of his family. But I will never understand how their suffering, or yours, or mine, is transformed into love: There is an alchemy of the spirit forever hidden in the depths of the human heart.

Meditate for a moment on these words. They sit quietly on page 39 of the book you hold in your hands, but if you let them into your heart, they will break it:

"On December 1, 1941, SS *Standartenfuehrer* Jaeger, Commandant of *Einsatzgruppe* 3, reported to his superiors his satisfaction over the completion of the initial phase of his task. Between June 22 and December 1, 137,346 Jews had been killed in Lithuania, among them 11 members of my family."

Mindless cruelty, sweeping devastation, utter impotence in the face of evil: I do not know how a human being arises from such ashes with his or her humanity not only intact but enhanced. But I know it must be done, for if it is not we will spiral down more and more rapidly towards humankind's worst potentials and most tragic fate. And I know it can be done, for in this book I have learned about a man who did it in the midst of great evil—and in its author I know a man who did it in evil's wake.

When the residents of the Kovno Ghetto called upon Dr. Elkhanan Elkes to be their leader—entrusting him with the administration of their communal life, and in daily dealings with the Nazi death machine—he initially refused, partly out of modesty and partly out of a sense of inadequacy: "His field was medicine, and medicine only." But he soon accepted this awesome burden because, as his son writes, "he knew who he was."

Dr. Elkhanan Elkes knew what his values were, values rooted in the sanctity of human life—and he knew that those values must prevail over Nazi nihilism. He knew that he was not a man alone but a man embedded in community—and he knew that the common good must take precedence over individual survival. His story is that of a moral and spiritual giant who dared to lead, and continued to lead, against impossible odds, who never lost faith in his community—or in the common humanity that binds us all.

This book is an important contribution to the historical record of the bloody twentieth century. But it cannot and should not be read as history alone. We honor the memory of those who suffered, and the author's deepest intentions, only by reading this story as our story—as a light thrown on the evil of our own place and time, as a challenge to find our own courage to confront and defy that evil. This is spiritual literature of the highest sort, calling us to resist with love the powers of darkness around us and within us.

I am deeply blessed to know Joel Elkes and call him friend, and his invitation to say a few words at the outset of this book is the finest honor I have received in thirty years as a writer. Indeed, we are all honored to share this earth with Dr. Elkhanan Elkes, his family, and his community of resistance—and there is a way we can return the honor.

If we who read this book are willing to learn more about ourselves even as we learn more about these remarkable people—willing to let their witness rid us of the fearful and ignoble habit of ignoring the evil around us—then the suffering this book records will be transformative. This book, and the spirit that infuses it, call us to embody the abiding grace, deep compassion, and active, outreaching love that the world so desperately needs.

Parker J. Palmer
Madison, Wisconsin
August, 1999

Preface

On November 19, 1997, there opened, at the U.S. Holocaust Museum in Washington D.C., a major exhibition on the Kovno Ghetto, the community led by Dr. Elkhanan Elkes.

Some four years in preparation, it documents, in much greater detail than is possible in a short Memoir, the story of this book. The opening was attended by nearly one thousand people, including many survivors and their families.

It is hard to convey with equanimity the extraordinary display of affection for Dr. Elkes which was manifested during this meeting. Again and again persons I did not know, or whom I only dimly remembered from my youth, came up to me to share this or that detail of their encounter with my father. Notes, messages, even the copy of an old prescription written by Dr. Elkes, were pressed into my hand. Warm letters and gifts followed throughout the year. I cannot thank them all; but particularly recall a magnificent pair of tall wooden candlesticks—carved in memory of Dr. Elkes by Mr. Morris Rich, renowned founder of a major woodworking studio in Miami. Mr. Rich had worked in the Ghetto woodworking shop in his teens, and had been with Dr. Elkes during his final days in Landsberg-Dachau Concentration Camp. The candlesticks arrived complete with memorial candles in place.

Since the opening, one and a half million people have seen the exhibition. A major museum publication* recalls and documents the march of events from 1941 to 1944. Educational materials have gone out to groups teaching Holocaust history in schools and universities. A two-hour documentary film, *Kovno Ghetto—A Buried History*, commissioned by the History Channel and narrated by Sir Martin Gilbert—noted historian and biographer of Churchill—was shown at the opening, and subsequently in Israel to much critical acclaim.

Joel Elkes
Fetzer Institute, July 1999

---

*   *The Hidden History of the Kovno Ghetto*, edited by Dennis B. Klein, U.S. Holocaust Museum (New York: Bullfinch Press, 1997), 255 pp.

Acknowledgments

I wish to acknowledge with deep gratitude the interest and encouragement I have received from friends. Avraham Tory read the original draft and checked it for historical accuracy, line by line, suggesting no less than 103 emendations. I am most grateful to him for the care he brought to the task, and for putting some photographs from his archives at my disposal. Sol Littman made some very helpful editorial suggestions and has been most generous in allowing me to quote from his book. It was a privilege to meet Esther Lurie in Israel in 1989. I had known her album *A Living Witness* since its publication in 1958. At our meeting she gave me a copy of a portrait of my father drawn in the Ghetto in 1943 (figure 26); and subsequently was very generous in sending me additional drawings, (figures 20, 21, 22, 23). I am very grateful to her and to her daughter, Mrs. Judith Shapiro-Clark for allowing me to reproduce these in this memoir.

I have not had the honor of meeing the late W.W. Mishell but, posthumously, wish to acknowledge my debt to him for his magnificent *Kaddish for Kovno* and to Mrs. Pola Mishell for permission to quote from his book. To our deep regret, the artist who drew Dr. Elkes on his deathbed (figure 27) remains unknown to us; he has our profound thanks.

My warm thanks also, to Mr. Jeffrey Czekaj and Mr. Jason Christian of Harvard University Press for permission to quote from the English edition of the Tory *Diary*, and the reproduction of one photograph.

In the early preparation of the lecture upon which this Memoir is based, I had the profound and steadfast support of my dear late first wife, Charmian, who had looked into the darkness long before I was able to do so; of my dear late second wife, Josephine; of Dr. Leah Dickstein, Mrs. Lonny Darwin, and Mr. Moissej Aronson. Mrs. Elizabeth Berman, Dr. Jack Brauns, Mr. Clive Burton, Mr. Terrence Elkes, Sir Martin Gilbert, Mr. Steven Goodell, Dr. Walter Reich, Ms. Myra Sklarew, and Mr. Jeshajahu Weinberg have all read the manuscript and given me their valuable suggestions. I have incorporated these to the best of my ability.

I want to express my heartfelt thanks to the Vice Chancellor of the University of Leicester, Dr. Kenneth J.R. Edwards, and the then Pro-Vice Chancellor, Professor Alan Ponter, for their continuing and unfailing support of the Elkhanan and Miriam Elkes Memorial Lectureship; to Mrs. Audrey Burton for founding the Stanley Burton Center for Holocaust Studies in the University of Leicester, which provided the setting for my lecture; to Professor Aubrey Newman, Director Emeritus of the Stanley Burton Center, for writing an editorial preface to the English Edition; to Mrs. Ilana Ash for permission to reproduce an extract from her letter to my sister (page 101) and a photograph in her possession (figure 4a); to Ms. Sharon Leighton and Mrs. Teresa Harrison for their patience and skill in typing the original manuscript; and to Mr. Patrick Armstrong of Vale Publishing (London) for the meticulous preparation of the English Edition.

It was Mr. Robert Lehman, President of the Fetzer Institute, who encouraged me to proceed with the publication of the book in the United States. His response was key in my resuming the initiative. Mrs. Phyllis Tickle of *Publishers Weekly* did me the immense kindness of introducing me to Dr. Lillian Miao of Paraclete Press. To her, and to her staff, I express my warm thanks for the care they have brought to the preparation of this book.

Editor's Note to the English Edition

Leadership in the Kovno Ghetto

In the pattern of Jewish life in Eastern Europe before 1939, an important part was played by the Jewish Councils and by individuals who played an important part in the leadership of their communities. However, with the coming of the war and the consequent disruption of all life in Poland, Jewish and non-Jewish alike, many of these leaders disappeared, and the communities were left floundering. At the same time, however, the new German administration decreed that the Jewish population should be concentrated into a number of ghettos, each administered by a Nazi-appointed *Judenrat* and each headed by a Jewish Elder. The decrees that established these institutions made it clear that the individuals who made them up had no option but to accept the office that was imposed upon them, and that they were personally and collectively "fully responsible" to the Nazi authorities for the "exact and punctual execution" of all orders delivered to them. The leaders who were brought forward through these decrees were often enough not the "natural" leaders of the community. Indeed, in many cases the Germans, when faced with leaders nominated by the Jewish communities, shot the first nominees and "invited" the communities to make a further set of choices. In other cases the Germans themselves nominated an individual who was to take over as the head of the Ghetto Council.

Over the next years these Councils had the task of organizing the daily life of the Jewish populations, of regulating rations, of allocating housing, and, in many cases, of ensuring the continuance of the hospitals, the orphanages, and all aspects of life. All relations between the German occupying authorities and the Jewish communities had to pass through the hands of these Councils, which had, in consequence, to establish a complete bureaucracy within the ghetto. Each ghetto was fully enclosed, and within the ghetto there was established a police force responsible for maintaining law and order as well as implementing the decrees of the Council.

As a consequence there has been a considerable argument among historians about the part played by such men as Jacob Gens of Vilna, of Adam Czerniakow of Warsaw, or of Chaim Rumkowski of Lodz. Some writers have maintained that without their willingness to obey German orders, however reluctant such acquiescence might have been, it would not have been possible for the Germans to have implemented the Final Solution. Others have pointed to the ways in which such leaders did their best to establish some order for the populations placed under their guidance, and that their aim was to try to preserve as many as possible in the hope that eventually some would survive the war and continue a pattern of Jewish life. Over the past few years, as a result of the work of historians such as Adam Trunk, Israel Guttman, and Yehuda Bauer, a great deal of light has been thrown upon the agonies faced by these leaders.

There was, however, one important difference between the ghettos of the part of Poland occupied by the Germans in 1939 and those that came under German control after June 1941. The full horrors of German occupation had not developed immediately in Poland, but the ghettos further east, and above all in Lithuania, were established only after the initial waves of massacres conducted by the local populations, but instigated by the German armies and *Einsatzgruppen* immediately after the German invasions. The Jewish leadership could have had no illusions about what was to happen to them, while the members of the Jewish communities who had survived the first wave of massacres were also only too aware of what had been happening around them.

It is in this atmosphere that the Jews of Kovno were instructed to appoint a leader, and it is under these circumstances that Elkhanan Elkes eventually allowed his name to go forward. Avraham Tory's diary shows very clearly the debates that took place and the procedures as a result of which Dr. Elkes received a vote of confidence from his leading contemporaries. It was to be this fact, however, that marked him out among the leaders of the ghettos of Eastern Europe. He had not sought office, but rather it was forced upon him. On the other hand, it was not forced upon him by the occupying forces, but rather by the Jews themselves. There can be no clearer statement of Elkes's unique position than that made by an eminent Rabbi of the Community:[1]

> How terrible is our position that we are not offering the revered Dr. Elkes the respected position of Head of the Jewish Community of Kovno but the shameful and humiliating one of "Head of the Jews," who is to represent us before the Germans. But please understand, dear and beloved Dr. Elkes, that only to the Nazi murderers will you be "Head of the Jews." In our eyes you will be the head of our community, elected in our most tragic hour, when blood runs from all of us and the murderer's sword is suspended over our heads. It has fallen to your part to accept duties of unequalled difficulty, but at the same time it is also a great privilege and a deed of charity, and you do not have the right to escape from it; stand at our head, defend us: You shall be with us and we will be with you until we arrive at the great day of salvation.

If that was the way in which Elkes was appointed the representative leader of the Jews of Kovno, the works of Avraham Tory and of William Mishell illustrate very clearly the ways in which he fulfilled the responsibilities laid upon him. Over and over they show the ways in which, at very real danger to his own life, he maintained his principles and did his best to defend his community. And he had always the moral advantage that, compared with the others in similar positions, he had no personal ambitions. These works illustrate clearly Dr. Elkes's moral ascendancy. Those who teach the history of Eastern Europe in these years have always had the responsibility of trying to understand what led the Jewish leaders to act as they did. At the same time it has always been important that we have had the example of Elkhanan Elkes to set beside the others.

We at Leicester were pleased that Sara Elkes agreed to establish here an annual lecture in memory of her father and to link it with the memory of her mother, for it was clear how important was her support to her husband. It was fitting also that the initial lecture was delivered by Professor Joel Elkes as a personal tribute. All who were present on that occasion were aware of the personal strain and emotion that this lecture represented for both of them. But it was a fitting tribute to a man who all feel had accepted an awesome challenge and met it bravely, who at the time when the ghetto was destroyed down, emerged untarnished, having preserved the lives of a significant number of its inhabitants.

Aubrey Newman
Director Emeritus
The Stanley Burton Center
for Holocaust Studies
University of Leicester

I
Introduction

When my sister, Sara Elkes, the founder of this Lectureship, suggested that I deliver the lecture on which this Memoir is based, I acceded at once. Yet, within hours, the full implications of this brotherly impulse surfaced in their stark truth. It is not easy, in any circumstances, to speak in public of one's parents. The hidden treasures of youth are private, and, to retain their magic, of necessity must remain private. The public events that have made Dr. Elkes a major figure in the history of the Holocaust were events at which I was not present. I was therefore at a double disadvantage. A loyal son is not the best of witnesses; and in any event, I am only a witness once removed. There is also the inner silence that the mind observes in the face of the unthinkable and unspeakable. In my own case my moratorium with myself lasted for more than two decades. In this respect I find I am not alone. The authors I quote worked through a similar predicament.[2,3]

Yet, despite the above reservations, I am glad of the opportunity. For my purpose is to connect the person I knew and remember with the person I have learned to know from the accounts of others, and to relate this person to the life, death, and destiny of the community that he served and led. The outlines of the story I am about to tell are slowly becoming known. Those unfamiliar with it I refer to my own principal sources: Avraham Tory's *Diary* (of some 550 pages, published in English translation by Harvard University Press in 1990),[2] with a comprehensive and searching introduction by Sir Martin Gilbert and invaluable historical notes by Professor Dina Porat; William Mishell's unforgettable *Kaddish for Kovno*;[3] and Sol Littman's *War Criminal on Trial: The Rauca Case*.[4] There are other major accounts in Hebrew, particularly that of Dr. Leib Garfunkel,[5] a key member of the Ghetto Council, and by Rabbi Ephraim Oshry.[6] Personal conversations, letters, tape recordings, and archival documents in my own possession or put at my disposal most generously by Mr. Tory have added to my knowledge, which, to this day, however, remains grossly incomplete. Every month brings new details; these are for others to record.

There are four main parts to this Memoir. The first introduces six persons; the second deals with the carnage that preceded and followed the German occupation of Lithuania in the summer of 1941; the third recounts the survivors' response to ruthless oppression and planned murder; and the fourth tells of the final phase of the Final Solution. I also add some afterthoughts.

2
Persons

There are, as noted, six persons who occupy a central place in the story I am about to tell. They are my parents, Elkhanan and Miriam Elkes; Lucy Elstein-Lavon; Esther Lurie; and Avraham and Pnina Tory.

Elkhanan and Miriam Elkes

My father, Elkhanan Elkes, was born in 1879 in Kalvarija, a little township some 35 miles from Kovno, Lithuania.[7] He was the second of six children. His father kept a small general store which, as I recall from my childhood, always smelled of a mix of carbolic soap, kerosene, spices, and salted herring. Here—skullcap in place and frockcoat meticulously brushed, his beard carefully trimmed—my grandfather, Israel Meir Elkes, would move among the barrels and boxes and bags of flour, sugar, and cattle feed, serving his peasant customers with exquisite good manners and humor. In the back of the store was his small study, to which he would retire to dwell on his beloved Talmud. And here—so the story goes—there could at times be seen a handsome red-headed boy reading the encyclopedia in Russian. It is reported that young Elkhanan started with the letter A and simply went on. Nobody knows which high school he attended or how he did there, or how, for that matter, he graduated from the University of Koenigsberg, across the border from Lithuania, in East Prussia. But graduate he did, with distinction in Medicine, in 1903. I still have his thesis on the "Structure of the Thyroid Gland at the Time of Birth." He continued to work as an assistant in the University clinic in both medicine and surgery, supplementing his income by tutoring. It was as her tutor that he met and wooed his future wife, Miriam Malbin.

The outbreak of World War I saw him a medical officer in the Russian Army, moving with his regiment from the Oder to the Urals and back again. He weathered the Russian Revolution in the small town of Orsha. Even then his house provided shelter to White Russians and Commissars alike. In 1919 or 1920—I do not know which—he returned to the country of his birth, settling in Kovno (Kaunas), the temporary capital of the newly declared independent Lithuanian Republic. There he established his practice as an internist. It grew and grew. Very rapidly he became the leading physician of the land, counting the President, the Prime Minister, and the Diplomatic Corps among his patients. With Dr. Berman and Dr. Brauns he built the Division of Internal Medicine in the newly founded Jewish Hospital. With Dr. Moshe

Schwabe—later Rector of the Hebrew University in Jerusalem—and a few others, he established a secondary school—the Hebrew Gymnasium, *Gymnassion Ivry Kovno*, a school in which all subjects were taught in Hebrew, and which later trained some of the brightest future educators and leaders of Israel. Yet he kept away from committees and councils. To the core he was, and remained, a private person.

As I write, I recall his clean features and his smile. His movements were small and graceful. He rarely raised his voice in public, but when he spoke there was warmth and interest and humor in it, qualities that gave anyone in his presence a sense of closeness and courage. Human frailty—including his own—was to him part of the Almighty's prescription for a good and full life. Only in the presence of bigotry, prejudice, and cruelty would his demeanor change. He would then grow silent, and his silence was often followed by a statement of such devastating directness as to render his hearer dumbfounded and confused. It was, for example, well known in his Russian regiment that antisemitic remarks in the officers' mess were definitely not worthwhile in the presence of Dr. Elkes. On the other hand, he sometimes used to tell me, with a genuine—almost childlike—delight, of his discussions on Judaism with the British or German or Russian Ambassador.

He was generous to a fault. His waiting room was always full of patients who could not pay, and so was his ward in the Jewish Hospital. Although easily approachable to these patients, he kept his distance with others. It is reported, for example, that when the wife of the Prime Minister called him on a Saturday to ask to see him, he politely inquired whether it was urgent. Being reassured that it was not, he suggested simply: "It is my Sabbath. However, I would be very glad to see you tomorrow or on Monday."

In times of crisis, his counsel was sought by wielders of power; yet, as noted above, he took the greatest pains to avoid any public office—even service on the boards of the school and the hospital he had helped to found.

On his desk there rested a little tablet carrying an inscription taken from the grave of Emmanuel Kant, who was buried in Koenigsberg. "Two things," it said (I am translating from memory), "continue to astonish the mind, the more it dwells upon them. One is the starry sky above me, and the other the moral law within me."

Elkhanan Elkes really lived these questions and shared them with his children. I still recall conversations and wonderful letters written in classical Hebrew while I was a university student. I last saw him at the railway station in Kovno in the summer of 1938.

His wife, Miriam, whom he wooed and married while teaching her Hebrew in Koenigsberg, was the daughter of a moderately prosperous grain merchant, Moses Malbin, and his wife Esther. Blessed with warmth, vitality, and curiosity, and extraordinarily well read, she assimilated the best of German and French culture, while always drawing on the wellsprings of her Jewish heritage. Much of what she had learned was self-taught. Her cheerful temperament complemented my father's sometimes somber mood. She was his complete confidante and life companion. She was a wonderful mother, a fount of joy, optimism, adventure, and sheer lifemanship, and she was full of sound, practical advice. I still treasure some of her letters from my student days, written in impeccable copperplate.

The formidable strength and spiritual reserves of this extraordinary woman did not become apparent until the last years of her life. Countless persons have related to Sara and me how they drew on Mrs. Elkes's strength in the ghetto, in the camp, and beyond.

Lucy Elstein-Lavon

Lucy Elstein, who became the secretary of the Kovno Ghetto Council, was the daughter of a charming couple who kept a fragrant-smelling pharmacy on Main Street in Kovno. Fluent in German, Lithuanian, Russian, Hebrew, and Yiddish, working closely with Avraham Tory from the beginning of the establishment of the Ghetto, and, later—at Dr. Elkes's and the Council's urging—in the Gestapo office, she proved an extraordinary source of intelligence during some of the most critical times in the Ghetto. It was she who, typing memoranda and orders through fresh carbons (which could subsequently be read), passed on information of value to the Council. She was one of the last people to leave Kovno Ghetto. After deportation and a terrible imprisonment in

Stutthof Concentration Camp—where she was with my mother—she came to the then Palestine via Italy. There she married a giant of modern Israel, Pinchas Lavon. It is hard to convey even remotely the closeness of the ties that bound my mother, my sister, Sara, me, and Avraham and Pnina Tory to Lucy. She died in Israel in 1982.

Esther Lurie

Esther Lurie was born in Libau, Latvia, and trained as an art student in Brussels. She came to Palestine in 1934, to be recognized rapidly as a widely acclaimed artist and designer, and winning the coveted Dizengoff Award in 1938. As fate would have it, she visited relatives in Kovno in 1939 and was overtaken by events, becoming a captive of the Russians and, later, the German occupation. From the inception of the Ghetto in 1941, she became its "living witness," its unforgettable graphic chronicler. Her records of the unimaginable—drawn in pen, often within hours of an "Action"—recall Goya's *Horrors of War*. It is hard to fathom whence she drew the strength to put down what she witnessed. Only some 30 paintings out of around 200 of her works survived. They were hidden by Avraham Tory and taken out clandestinely with other documents. Her album *A Living Witness*,[8] taken together with Mr. George Kadushin's formidable photographic records—now exhibited in the Holocaust Museum in Washington—is one of the most precious archives of the Ghetto in existence. Her drawing of Dr. Elkes (figure 26), done in 1943, was given to me at a gathering of survivors. After going through concentration camps in Germany and Poland and being liberated by the Red Army, she returned to Palestine in 1945. She received a second Dizengoff Prize in 1946 and the Zussman Award in 1992, and has exhibited extensively in Israel and abroad. Several documentaries record her work. As she says in one of them: "Never did I think that the skills which I acquired in copying Rembrandt and Dürer would be put to such use." She died in Israel in 1998.

Avraham and Pnina Tory

Avraham Tory—or Avraham Golub, as he was then known—was born in the Lithuanian village of Lazdijai in 1909. His father had qualified as a rabbi; his mother's family were farmers. He studied at the Hebrew school in Marijampole, in which all subjects (as in my school) were taught in Hebrew.

The Zionist ideal—the return of the Jews to Palestine—was to him, as to many of us at the time, a very practical one. He rose rapidly in the Zionist youth movement and to this day remains one of the most senior members of the Maccabi Sports Association, having literally carried its flag in many countries.[9] He briefly studied law in the United States and completed his studies in Lithuania in 1933. Because of the restricted admission of Jews into the legal profession, he found himself barred from practice. He clerked for a Lithuanian judge (who had graduated at the same time as he) and later became assistant to Professor Simon Beliatskin, a Professor of Civil Law and a famous jurist—one of the few Jews on the faculty in Kovno. During the Russian occupation of Lithuania (between 1940 and 1941), he was employed by the Soviet military construction administration.

However, having been dismissed, and learning that he was to be deported because of his known Zionist activities, Tory went into hiding, only to return on June 22, 1941, on the eve of the German attack on Lithuania and the Soviet Union. That day, or, to be precise, at midnight of that day, Avraham Tory embarked on the task that ensures him a lasting place in Jewish history. Writing in the home of his sister and brother-in-law, Basja and Benjamin Romanovski, he recorded the awesome events of the day when several hundred Jews were brutally murdered in Kovno and its environs by roaming Lithuanian mobs. From then on he set down his testimony as often as he could, usually within a day or so of the events, until the last entry in his diary, some two years and nine months later, on January 9, 1944. The sparseness, economy, and stark detail of his writing only heighten the dimensions of the unfathomable tragedy he set himself to record. For it is one thing to write a diary—even in a prisoner-of-war camp; it is a totally different matter to keep a record of the day when you do not know whether you will survive into the following day. Yet, day by day, he acted on his iron determination to testify unto future generations. In Hebrew we have a name for the highest and most solemn prayer: We call it *Avodath Kodesh*—Holy Work. Without knowing or intending it, Avraham Tory did something of this holy work day by day.

Except for Dr. Elkes, Dr. Garfunkel, and the underground leader Hirsch Levin, none of the other members of the Council knew about the diary. A hiding place was needed. Pnina Sheinson—who as Pnina Ushpitz was my school friend, and who was later to become Mrs. Tory—offered to hide the material, despite grave danger to herself and her little daughter Shulamith. Two boys were used as messengers to deliver the pages and documents day by day. When, at times, Avraham Tory was on the verge of collapse, it was his future wife's urgings that kept him going. Tory would dictate the entries and Pnina would write them down. This process explains why some parts of the diary are in her handwriting.

Documentary materials were added to the diary almost daily, and the archives grew rapidly. A safe place for their storage had to be found. The story of the diary and its accompanying documents, their retrieval, their travels through four countries with the Torys or in the trust of friends, is a tale that must be told unabridged to fathom its full depth and meaning. Sir Martin Gilbert records it in his introduction to Tory's book:[10] I can only give you a few facts.

The documents, wrapped in greaseproof paper, were packed into five wooden crates and encased in metal sheeting, welded tight for safekeeping. One of the crates contained Tory's last will and testament. The crates were then buried deep below the concrete foundations of a three-story building known as Block C. Only three people—Avraham Tory, Pnina Sheinson, and Shraga Goldschmidt, who had fashioned the crates—knew their hiding place.

On November 22, 1943, Avraham Tory clandestinely took Pnina Sheinson and her daughter Shulamith out of the Ghetto; and, with the help of the great and valiant Lithuanian priest Bronius Paukstys, mother and daughter were hidden in a distant peasant's home through the winter. Shulamith was quite ill at the time. Responding to pleas, the peasant family finally agreed to accept Avraham Tory as well. On March 23, 1944, carrying my father's last letter and testament to Sara and me (see page 88), Tory escaped from the Ghetto and remained in hiding with Pnina and Shulamith until the German withdrawal in 1944. They returned to Kovno and were married there on August 10. Kovno, by that time, was again under Russian occupation. The KGB knew of the existence of the documents, and friends urged the Torys to surrender the material, which was endangering their safety and, possibly, their lives.

To their immense credit, and the credit of Jewish poet and writer Avraham Sutzkever, who urged them to hold on, the Torys did not give up or give in. Working in the dead of night, they and their friend Shraga Goldschmidt recovered with great difficulty three of the five crates from the ruins of the building where they had been buried; the other two had sunk too deep because of soil subsidence. The material was transferred to three satchels. Like a sacred text, it never left the Torys, or those to whom it was entrusted. Months later, it was taken to Israel. The originals are still in the Torys' possession.

Avraham Tory told me, years later, that he did not look at the material for many months—indeed years. It was, he said, like "touching fire." For myself, I recall a particular visit to Israel in 1956 when I learned of the existence, and implications, of the *Diary*. I had been asked to lecture at the Weizmann Institute, and my plane was to leave the following morning. That night, after the lecture, I stayed up with Avraham and Pnina until 1:00 A.M., while, in document after document, he shared his riveting evidence. We could not possibly finish, and he insisted on coming to the airport.

Early the following morning, colleagues and staff from the Weizmann Institute were there to see me off. Very soon Avraham appeared, with a bulging blue satchel. Oblivious of my guests, we sat in the tiny airport hut—that was all it was at the time—drinking Russian tea, while Avraham went on reminiscing loudly about this and that person whom we had known at school or in the community. My hosts were taken aback; and when we told them that we were talking about the Holocaust, and friends whom we had lost, they seemed even more bewildered. Yet, as Avraham and I talked, as we remembered faces, smiles, pranks, and other tales of youth, we suddenly broke out into loud laughter. From then on we could speak of the unspeakable.

Somewhere around that time, too, Avraham began to organize his material and prepare it for publication. This took time, and the first rough draft was not ready until 1984 or 1985. The Hebrew version was published by Tel Aviv University in 1988.[11] Dr. Jack Brauns—now a resident of Los Angeles—who had been in the Ghetto, and whose father, Dr. Moses Brauns, had functioned with rare distinction as physician in the Ghetto (see page 74), put Avraham Tory in touch with Sir Martin Gilbert. It is he, Dr. Jack Brauns, and I who were responsible for the publication of the English edition.

These, then, are the six persons whom Sara and I knew, and who will, from time to time, appear in the tale that I am about to tell: Some of these appearances, of necessity, will be very brief. I can only hope to give you glimpses of events, flashes of a searchlight. In the Holocaust, carnage goes by the name of "Actions." This Memoir is about the survival of people in the face of such "Actions."

3
Carnage: The Beginning [4, 11, 12, 13, 14]

Tory's first entry of June 22, 1941, records the events of that day.[12]

"On June 22, 1941, residents of Kovno woke up to a bitter surprise. Instead of the usual diet of light music, the radio was broadcasting unusual and ominous news from Moscow." At a number of points, German troops had attacked Red frontier guards, and had crossed the border into Lithuania. Heavy bombing raids on military bases, on the central railway station of Kovno, and on other parts of the town confirmed the outbreak of war.

By the afternoon of the first day of the German advance, Soviet officials were in full flight, having requisitioned most of the taxis and railroads to evacuate their families. Suddenly the Jews of Kovno found themselves abandoned, devoid of protection from either the army or the police. People rushed to the railway stations where they waited for trains that never came. Others set out by cart or on foot. The routes were dangerous. German fighters descended on the trudging masses, killing many and forcing the rest to take shelter. People abandoned their belongings or exchanged them for food. Families were torn asunder: Women and children were shot in the woods. Tory, returning from an attempted escape, describes the feeling: "Like a hunted animal in a forest going up in flames."[13]

The Germans entered Kovno on the night of June 24, but even before their entry the carnage had begun. Roaming bands were killing Jews wherever they found them. The German commander, SS Brigadier General Franz Stahlecker, impressed upon local leaders that their place in the greater Reich could be earned best by helping the Reich's sacred struggle against the Jews: Lithuanian agitators obliged.

The killings that ensued were unsurpassed in their ferocity and random cruelty. Within three days and nights of the Germans' arrival, some 3800 Jews had been murdered in Kovno and Slobotka (part of which was destined to become the Ghetto). Women and children were marched to the Seventh Fort—part of a ring of fortresses on the perimeter of the town—to be executed in front of freshly dug pits. Some 8000 Jews were killed during the first three weeks of German occupation.

It was not many weeks before General Stahlecker moved his headquarters to Riga, Latvia. In Kovno, he left behind Colonel Jaeger, commander of Operation Group 3 of the *Einsatzkommando*—the specialists in extermination. Working under Jaeger were Captain Heinrich Schmitz and Master Sergeant Helmut Rauca.[14] They were joined later by Alfred Tornbaum, commander of the Second Company of the Third Police Reserve Battalion.

As the days and months proceeded, Schmitz and Rauca emerged as the Jewish Affairs Specialists in "Region Kaunas." Their names haunt survivors to this day.

The German command liked order—*Ordnung*—in its death industry. The plan, as subsequently codified by Heydrich at the Wannsee conference (held in a Berlin Villa on January 20, 1942), was simple. There were to be four stages in carrying out the Final Solution: First *concentration;* second *segregation* according to fitness and exploitation through physical labor; third *extermination;* and, finally, physical *destruction* of the habitat. Over the next three years this plan was to proceed in Kovno with characteristic German efficiency; however, as will be noted, some unforeseen developments altered both the timetable and the course of the operation.

On July 7, 1941, a German staff car stopped in front of the house of the chief rabbi of Kaunas, Avraham Kahane Shapiro, and ordered him to come to headquarters. The rabbi, who was a prominent and revered figure in Lithuania, pleaded illness. Dissatisfied that the rabbi could not accompany him, the officer demanded that he appoint three prominent Jews to take his place. The rabbi nominated Leib Garfunkel, Jacob Goldberg, and Ephraim Rabinovitch for the unknown task. The rabbi had chosen wisely. Leib Garfunkel was a former member of the Lithuanian parliament; Jacob Goldberg was a soldier and officer and old friend of the high-ranking Lithuanian military; and Dr. Ephraim Rabinovitch was a prominent gynecologist who spoke fluent German. In their favor, too, was the fact that both Garfunkel and Goldberg had been arrested by the Communists during the occupation. Within the hour, these three were waiting in the anteroom of the Gestapo Chief. On Gestapo orders, Rabbi Snieg, former chaplain of the Lithuanian army, and Rabbi Schmukler joined them.

Two of the people present were Colonel Jaeger and SS General Pohl, head of the Waffen SS. There were only two chairs in the room. "You may sit as far as there are chairs." All delegates remained standing at the interview.

Jaeger began (I am condensing): "The Lithuanians hate you. They don't want you living among them. . . . They blame you for the Soviet invasions and for the deportations. . . . Things are out of control. . . . We Germans are responsible for order, and we cannot allow this wild situation to continue. You must move and withdraw into a place where we can protect you. You must move into a Ghetto." Jaeger then turned to a large map on the wall and pointed to the suburb across the river of Kaunas—to Viljampole, otherwise known as Slobotka. "This is where you'll go, and this is where you're going to establish your own municipality." Slobotka had been the site of Jewish settlements for a least four centuries. It was the site of a great Talmudic center, the Slobotka Yeshiva, which had trained many Talmudic luminaries. It was small. It had no sewers, no running water. The streets were unpaved. There were about 7000 residents living there who would have to be resettled in Kaunas. Clearly, it was far too small to accommodate the 30,000 Jews of the city. The delegation protested, requesting time to report to their community leaders, but to no avail. Jaeger demanded a response by 10:00 the following morning. Before the meeting ended, two conditions were set by the Jewish delegates. First, the slaughter on the Seventh Fort must stop; and second, the proposed Ghetto must be considerably enlarged. Jaeger is reported to have offered the release of 3000 women and children if his orders were followed.

At 10:00 A.M. sharp on the following day the delegation returned to Gestapo headquarters. They pleaded for a postponement of the evacuation, and for the inclusion of part of the old city of Kovno within the boundaries of the Ghetto. This plan, too, was refused.

In one respect, however, the delegation had won a point—namely, the inclusion of a block on the far side of Paneriu Street in the area of the Ghetto. This street was a major thoroughfare required for military traffic. For that reason, the Nazis suggested that access to the main Ghetto, the so-called big Ghetto, on the other side of Paneriu Street, be by a small footbridge that later on became a famous Ghetto landmark (see figure 14).

The transfer had to be accomplished within a month, between July 15 and August 15, 1941. Three thousand non-Jews who lived in Viljampole had to be evacuated.

The Lithuanian families were getting Jewish-owned apartments in the city in exchange. A small secretariat, consisting of two municipal employees and two nominees of the Jewish community, was appointed to develop an orderly plan for the evacuation. This was done under the direct supervision of the Mayor of Kaunas, Kazys Palciauskas, and the military governor, Bobelis. Three young lawyers, among them Avraham Golub, later to be known as Avraham Tory, volunteered their services to the Transfers Committee. Lucy Elstein, fluent in Yiddish, Lithuanian, and German, joined him as secretary.

The Civil Governor of Kaunas had one other demand: The Jewish community must elect its Head Jew—*Oberjude*—one who would act as chief of a Council of Elders, with whom he and his administration would deal. If the community did not do so within a matter of days, he would proceed to appoint one.

4
The Assembly [14, 15]

And so, on the night of August 4, 1941, a meeting was called at the Jewish schoolhouse at 24 Dauksos Street.[15] Seated in the small classroom were 28 of the most trusted members of the local Jewish community. The meeting was chaired by Dr. Grigory Wolff, whom I remember from my youth—a veteran leader of the Jewish community, director-general of Wolff Industries, and head of the Central Jewish Bank. Rising to his feet, he began in a faltering voice (I am paraphrasing from my conversation with Avraham Tory): "This is a historic gathering for the Kovno Jewish community. Never before have we faced such tragic circumstances. Never before have we suffered such tragic losses. We have been here before—more than once have we been on the brink of annihilation. However, the Jewish people know that every time a new Haman[16] arises to destroy us, he himself meets the same fate." At this point, Dr. Wolff faltered, put his hand to his head, sobbed, and had to be helped back to his seat.

The assembly considered a number of candidates for the position of *Oberjude*. Former officers in the Lithuanian army, former members of the Lithuanian Parliament, former bankers, Zionist leaders, and public figures were nominated. None of them won general approval; some feared the risk and burden of responsibility. None of them seemed to have the strength and stature to stand up to the Gestapo or to merit the unconditional trust of the whole community, in what was clearly a matter of life and death.

Avraham Tory recalls the pall that settled over the room. It was as if the Jewish community—previously proud of the quality and abundance of its leadership—had suddenly lost its way, at this most perilous moment. There was only one candidate no one was prepared to let go—Dr. Elkhanan Elkes. As Tory records: "His moral qualities, his familiarity with the German mentality, his strong bonds with the Jewish past, were recognized by everyone as making him the most fitting man for the job."[17]

Would he succeed in carrying the burden to the end, or would he collapse under its weight? "Modest man that he was," writes Tory, "Dr. Elkes demurred. He said he did not have experience in public administration, he knew nothing about housing, police, public safety, work, or social service. He had never engaged in this kind of work; his field was medicine, and medicine only. He absolutely refused and asked that his candidacy be dropped."

The leaders despaired. Little time remained, and still no man of the hour had emerged. Tory continues, "Everybody was oppressed at what could happen if we didn't appoint the people demanded by the authorities. It could only mean further bloodshed." There was a lengthy silence. And then, Rabbi Schmukler—rabbi of the Suburb of Sanciai—rose and made a statement that, in the annals of the Holocaust, has proven historic. Turning to Dr. Elkes, he said, "The Kovno Jewish community stands on the brink of disaster. Our daughters are being raped, our men are being murdered, and death is staring into our windows. Jews! The German authorities insist that we appoint an *Oberjude,* but what we need is a "Leader of the Community," a trustworthy servant of the public. The man most fitting for this position at this tragic moment is Dr. Elkes. We therefore turn to you and say: Dr. Elkes, you may be an *Oberjude* for whoever wants to regard you as such; but to us you will be Leader of our Community. We all know your path will be fraught with hardship and danger, but we will go with you all the way, and may God come to our aid. With your deep Jewish faith you will take us out of the Ghetto, this exile within exile, to our Holy Land. There you will be our true leader. We implore you, be our Community Leader—*Rosh Hakahal*—at this time. Be strong." And quoting an ancient Hebrew proverb, Rabbi Schmukler added, "Remember, messengers on behalf of the Commandments suffer no harm thanks to the Prayers of the Multitude." He closed, "Dr. Elkes, we beg of you, rise up and take over this leadership." There was not a dry eye in the room.

Pale and serious, Dr. Elkes rose. "If you are all of the opinion that, by accepting, I will render a service to the common good, then I accept." Immediately, the tension in the room broke. A feeling of euphoria overcame the assembly. People congratulated each other for having made such a fortunate choice. They shook Dr. Elkes's hand and embraced him. They linked arms and sang the Jewish anthem *Ha Tiqua,* which, translated into English, means *Hope.* Facing Dr. Elkes, arms raised high and palms extended, Rabbi Schmukler delivered the ancient benediction, "Go with our blessing."

5
Ghetto

D r. Elkes acted immediately, and, after short reflec-
tion, appointed Leib Garfunkel, a well-known
attorney, as his deputy. Michael Koppelman, the representative of Lloyd's of London in Lithuania, became
Chief of the Ghetto Police. Jacob Goldberg, Ephraim
Rabinovitch, Leon Rostovski, Hirsch Levin, and former
army chaplains Rabbi Snieg and Rabbi Schmukler were
also chosen to serve. Three young lawyers, Israel
Bernstein, Elimelech Kaplan, and Avraham Golub (Tory)
were appointed as Council secretaries. Their duties were
to keep the minutes of meetings, handle correspondence,
coordinate among various departments of the Council,
arrange transport, provide housing, and keep track of
food supplies for the Ghetto. Avraham Golub's duty was
to maintain contact with the civil town administration.
All were people of the greatest integrity.

Within days of Dr. Elkes's appointment, the trek to
the Ghetto began, so vividly described in Tory's diaries[18]
and in Mr. Mishell's recollections.[19] The Germans had

banned the use of non-Jewish cars, trucks, and even horse-drawn wagons, so families loaded their possessions on their backs, in baby carriages, on sledges made of doors, and in wheelbarrows, and moved them across the bridge. Representatives of the Council, in the meantime, had surveyed the Ghetto; when the people arrived they were greeted by them and assigned housing—there was an average of five to eight people to a room, or three square meters (a space about 5 feet by 6½ feet) per person.

Avraham Tory told me with particular poignancy of the day when the Germans entered my parents' apartment with a view to looting their possessions. He records Dr. Elkes's cold and polite contempt, offering this and that treasure—"perhaps this picture or this piece of crystal?"—to the uncomprehending looters. Tory ran up and down the stairs, loading the wagon; Dr. Elkes was extremely concerned about Avraham Tory's safety that day, until he saw him again later: It was a day of killing. This is how the friendship and collaboration between Dr. Elkes and Avraham Tory began.

Even during this transition, the shape of things to come became monstrously evident. All radios had to be turned in. Jews were not allowed any non-Jewish help. Jewish doctors were no longer allowed to treat non-Jewish patients, and gentile doctors were prohibited from treating Jews. On July 10, 1941, the order of the yellow star was published. A yellow star (exactly eight centimeters [just over three inches] wide) had to be sewn firmly on to a garment, on both front and back. Jews were forbidden to shop for food, except in special shops at special hours.

As day by day the trek to the Ghetto continued, the pogroms did not stop. On August 5 about 1000 Jews were murdered in the Seventh Fort.

By August 15, the barbed wire fences—erected by Jews—were in place. Ghetto Kovno was sealed from the outer world. The first phase of the Final Solution had been completed. A new city commissioner, Colonel Hans Cramer, was appointed, and was swift to respond to his new duties.

Yet, even as the transfer was in progress, both the Ghetto Police and the Ghetto Court were conceived and created. To the Germans, the Ghetto Police force was an instrument of policy. Its function was to warehouse Jews until their labor was no longer needed, and then collude in their destruction.

In the Ghetto, however, the Jewish Police became an agent of civic order and, later, of Jewish resistance. Police Chief Koppelman took the greatest care in the selection of his men. He recruited athletes, men with military training, schoolteachers, and youth leaders. Their oath of office, drafted by Tory, pledged them to "protect the lives and honor the rights of Ghetto inmates, even if it endangered their own lives." The great and fearless Hirsch Levin served as intermediary between the police and the underground. Unlike in other Ghettos, it later became a preferred form of punishment to be delivered to the Jewish Police. Much of the credit for this moral tone set by the police was due to Dr. Elkes, to Mr. Koppelman, and to the Ghetto Court that functioned under Professor Beliatskin—an internationally known jurist.

The Council was still naive in the deceptive ways of the Gestapo. By mid-August, Cramer informed the Council that he needed some 500 educated men to put the shabbily kept municipality archives in order. The Council responded promptly. They drew up a list of candidates and posted on the Ghetto wall a notice announcing an opportunity for work. On August 18, the streets leading out of the Ghetto were filled with young lawyers, engineers, chemists, journalists, teachers, and technicians, some with a diploma tucked under their arm in case their status as intellectuals was questioned. By the side of the Ghetto gate—on the free side—one of the recruits for this new job recognized Helmut Rauca. Like a wave his name swept through the crowd, and people began to retreat. However, before the day was over, 534 men had been rounded up, taken away onto trucks, and driven away. None of the 534 was ever seen again.

The following day, a Jewish laborer who had been employed in a work gang brought to the Council offices a small packet of identification papers, found in the grass not far from the Fourth Fort. The soiled personal documents clearly belonged to various members of the 534 who had been taken away the previous night. The grim education of the Council in the ways of the Gestapo had begun.

The Council could not bring themselves to believe that, within one day, 534 of the bravest and best had been sent to their deaths. They asked for a meeting with Colonel Jaeger. It was refused. Dr. Elkes asked Cramer to call on him, so as to clarify the fate of the young men. Cramer assured Dr. Elkes there was no cause for alarm. The men were being well fed and well housed, and would return home in a few weeks. It is clear from Tory's account that Dr. Elkes stood his ground. He told Cramer not to take him for a fool; the Council had evidence that the 534 had been liquidated at the Fourth Fort. Unable to go on denying their death, Cramer changed his story. All 534 had been shot for committing sabotage. He claimed they had poured gasoline over a supply of sugar in order to contaminate it. Clearly a lie.

As the days and weeks passed, the organization of the death industry became ever more evident. A division of labor appeared. There were quotas for labor and quotas for killing. At the head of labor affairs stood Jewish Affairs specialist Captain Fritz Jordan. Jewish slave brigades began to work on September 8. The murder of the Jews was not Jordan's direct responsibility.

Killing Jews, on the other hand, was the Gestapo's, and specifically Rauca's, business. This division—even competition—between slavers and killers did not escape the Ghetto administration.

The tactics became clearer over the months that followed: offer, promise, countermand, deny, demoralize, confiscate, use, exploit—and then kill. Give too little—

sow envy, distrust, hatred—and then kill. Destroy hospitals, ban schools, close, burn, and desecrate places of worship—and then kill. Go for the spirit, go for the body—and then kill. Leave them, in, I believe, Bismarck's phrase, "only their eyes to weep with."

On September 17, 1941, Jordan—the said Jewish Affairs Specialist for civil administration in Kaunas—ordered the distribution of 5000 work cards, so-called "Jordan certificates," or *Jordanscheine*, to skilled workers through the Ghetto Council. A slip of the tongue on the telephone alerted the Council to the true meaning of these. An irate official called, asking them to issue *Lebensscheine*, "Life Certificates," to his brigade of workers. Immediately, the Council knew that these were, indeed, survival certificates; as rumors spread, terrible waves of anger, fury, and despair swept through the Ghetto. Howling crowds met outside the Ghetto administration building. The administration was invaded and ransacked for the precious certificates, accusations being made that the Council kept them for themselves. This chaos, of course, produced a reaction. Next morning, Lithuanian troops and police with machine guns surrounded the Ghetto. There was panic, fear of another Action. It passed, however, but proved merely a prelude to something much, much bigger in the weeks to come.

On October 4, 1500 Jews—including Dr. Elkes's brother and sister—were massacred on the Ninth Fort. On October 4, with all doors and windows barred and with 67 patients and Dr. Davidowicz still inside, the

Infectious Disease Hospital was set on fire. It burned all day and all night. The fire brigade was not allowed to put out the blaze. Dr. Zacharin, head of the hospital, my father's brother, Dr. Hirsch Elkes, Dr. Moses Brauns, and his son Dr. Jack Brauns (who went through the Ghetto and now lives in Los Angeles), were saved by a freak event.[20] Later that month, the Ghetto synagogue was savaged. Cats and dogs were thrown in, shot, and left to rot. Removal of the carcasses was punishable by death.

6
The Ninth Fort

Tory's next major entry was made on October 28, 1941.[21] Beyond the grasp of most, the original notes were written on the night of that awesome day. Subsequently, more material was added. My quotations draw on the diary and on Littman's account;[22] other material, based on conversations with Avraham Tory, is also included.

On Friday afternoon, October 24, a Gestapo car entered the Ghetto. It carried the Gestapo Deputy Chief, Captain Schmitz, and Master Sergeant Rauca. Their appearance filled all onlookers with fear. The Council was readied and ordered the Ghetto Police to follow all their movements. . . . Those movements were rather unusual. . . . Instead of calling at the Council offices, they toured various places, as if looking for something, tarried a while at Democracy Square, looked it over, leaving in their wake an ominously large question mark. What were they scheming to do?

The next day, October 25, a Saturday afternoon, Rauca, accompanied by a high Gestapo officer, came to see the Council. He did not waste any time. He opened with a major pronouncement: "It is imperative to increase the size of the Jewish labor force, in view of its importance for the German war effort." He, Rauca, intended to increase the rations for both the workers and their families. To forestall competition and envy, the active labor force would be separated from the less active; those less active would be transferred to the small Ghetto. To carry out the operation, a roll call would take place. The Council was to issue an order in which the Ghetto inmates, without exception, and irrespective of sex or age, were called to report to Democracy Square at 6:00 A.M. on the dot on October 28. In the square, they should line up by families and by the workplace of the family head. In meeting for the roll call, they were to leave their apartments, closets and drawers open. Anybody found in his home after 6:00 would be shot on the spot.

The members of the Council were shaken. What did this mean? Dr. Elkes attempted to get Rauca to divulge some information. He refused to add another word, and, accompanied by his associate, left the Council office.

The members of the Council remained in a state of shock. What lay in wait for the Ghetto? What was the true purpose of the roll call? Why did Rauca order the Council to publish the order rather than publish it himself? Was he planning to abuse the trust the Ghetto population placed in its Jewish leadership? If so, was it right for the Council to comply with Rauca's order, to become an accomplice to an act that might spell disaster? Was the Council entitled to take responsibility for the outcome of *not* publishing the order? An intermediary was contacted to inform Rauca that Dr. Elkes had requested another meeting with him.

To keep the meeting secret, it took place in Dr. Elkes's tiny dwelling. Dr. Elkes began by saying that his responsibilities as a leader of the community and a human being obliged him to speak openly of the fears that prevailed. And since the Germans' operational intention was only to order food distribution, the Council was prepared to carry out faithfully the appropriate decree. Therefore, he went on to say, there is no need for the roll call of the entire Ghetto, including elderly people and babes in arms, since such a summons was likely to cause panic. Moreover, the three roll calls that had taken place over the past three months had each ended in terrible Actions. Rauca feigned amazement that any suspicion at all could have been harbored by the members of the Council. He repeated his promise that a purely administrative matter was involved, and no evil intention lurked behind it. Dr. Elkes then appealed to the conscience of the Gestapo officer—*Wissen und Gewissen* (his Knowledge and Conscience)—hinting casually that every war, including the present one, comes to an end, and that, if Rauca answered questions openly, without concealing anything, the Jews would remember. Thus, Tory noted—as early as 1941 and, as will be seen later, not for the last time—Dr. Elkes intimated possible defeat of Germany in war, leaving Rauca a way to save his skin if he helped. Rauca remained unmoved. There were no hidden plans, no ill intentions behind the decree. He concluded the meeting and left.

In the meantime, other rumors had begun to circulate. Lithuanians reported that the Russian prisoners-of-war were digging large pits at the Ninth Fort. They were labeled "tank traps"; but when Rauca announced the roll call decree, these rumors and the roll call no longer seemed a coincidence. For hour upon hour the Council deliberated and could not reach an agreement. Would issuing the announcement be colluding with the Germans? Would not issuing the order invite savage retribution? Such was their anguish that they decided to seek the advice of Chief Rabbi Shapiro. At 11:00 P.M., Drs. Elkes, Garfunkel, Goldberg, and Levin set out for the rabbi's house. It took three meetings before the rabbi could give them counsel. In studying and interpreting his sources, he had found that there had been situations in Jewish history which resembled the dilemma the Council was facing now. In such cases, he said, he had found that when an evil edict imperiled the Jewish community and, by a certain act, part of the community could be saved, communal leaders were bound to summon their courage, take the responsibility, and save as many lives as they possibly could. According to this principle, it was incumbent on the Council to publish the decree. Reading it in retrospect, this seemed to have been the guiding principle of the Ghetto Council. If part of the community could be saved, community leaders were bound to summon their courage and their responsibility to save as many lives as possible.

Accordingly, the Ghetto Council published the announcement summoning every man, woman, and child to Democracy Square at 6:00 the following morning. However, it headed the edict with the significant phrase, "The Council has been ordered by the authorities," lest there be any misunderstanding as to the origin of the fateful announcement.

To grasp what follows, you must read Tory's account. "Tuesday morning, October 28, was a rainy day,"[23] he reports. "A heavy mist covered the sky, and the whole Ghetto was shrouded in darkness. A fine sleet filled the air and covered the ground in a thin layer. From all directions, dragging themselves heavily and falteringly, groups of men, women, and children, the elderly and the sick, leaning on the arms of their relatives or neighbors, babies carried in their mothers' arms, proceeded in long lines. They were all wrapped in winter coats, to protect themselves against the cold. Many families stepped along slowly, holding hands, all making their way to Democracy Square. It was a procession of mourners, grieving for themselves. Some 30,000 people proceeded that morning into the unknown, towards a fate that could already have been sealed for them by their rulers."

At 9:00 A.M. the Gestapo entourage appeared in the square—Deputy Chief Captain Schmitz, Master Sergeant Rauca, Captain Jordan, and Captain Thornbaum, accompanied by a squad of German policemen and Lithuanian collaborators. Rauca positioned himself on a little mound. His glance ranged briefly over the column of Council members and Jewish Ghetto Police and, by a movement of the hand, he motioned them to the left, which, as it became clear, was the "good" side. Then he signaled with a baton held in his hand, and ordered the remaining columns forward. The selection had begun.

This selection proceeded without stopping until nightfall, Rauca, from time to time, feasting on a sandwich or puffing on a cigarette. Again and again, Dr. Elkes tried to intervene, responding to cries and appeals, moving this family, this group, this person from right to left. As Tory reports,[24] "Dr. Elkes stood there, his face bearing an expression of bottomless grief; since 6:00 A.M., this 65-year-old man had been standing on his feet, refusing to sit on the stool that had been brought to him. Now and then, when he was overcome by a fit of weakness, those near him asked him to sit down, to regain his strength, or offered him a piece of bread. He refused, muttering. "Thank you, thank you, gentlemen; terrible things are happening here; I must remain standing on guard, in case I can be of assistance." Finally, on the next day (October 29) Dr. Elkes obtained permission from Rauca to enter the small Ghetto to save another hundred people. There, however, the guards fell upon him.

Savaged, trampled, and beaten with rifle butts, he fell to the ground unconscious, bleeding profusely from a head wound. Jewish policemen, onlookers, and Tory carried him on their shoulders into the nearest house in the big Ghetto, where he lay for three days. His head wounds were stitched, and he was nursed until he was able to return home. His effort to save a small number of Jews had almost cost him his life.

In the meantime, while he was lying unconscious, a procession numbering some 9200 people proceeded from the small Ghetto to the Ninth Fort. It lasted from dawn until noon. Upon arrival, people were immediately set upon, stripped of every valuable article, and then forced naked into the pits that had been prepared in advance. Machine guns positioned above the pits did the rest. The murderers—Lithuanian and German—did not have time to shoot everybody in one batch before the next batch arrived. The carnage continued until the quota of some 9200 men and women and children had been met in full.[25]

This Action has a sequel. In the autumn of 1943, the Germans, conscious of the Russian advance, began destroying the evidence of their killing on the Ninth Fort. They ordered the removal of the bodies from the mass graves, and their burning. A special prisoners' detail from the Ghetto—on special rations—was charged with this gruesome task.

On December 25—Christmas Day, 1943—following a plan conceived by a Russian prisoner, Captain

Vassilenko—which involved sawing through bars over several months, forcing a lock in a storeroom door, and using white sheets to obscure footsteps in the snow once outside—64 prisoners escaped from the Ninth Fort. Some of them found their way to the Ghetto, and subsequently joined the partisans in the Vilna forests.

On December 1, 1941, SS *Standartenfuehrer* Jaeger, Commandant of *Einsatzgruppe* 3, reported to his superiors his satisfaction over the completion of the initial phase of his task. Between June 22 and December 1, 137,346 Jews had been killed in Lithuania, among them 11 members of my family.

7
Work

On October 29, as the Germans and their Lithuanian collaborators were still shooting Jews on the Ninth Fort, not one of the Jewish slave labor brigades showed up at the gate for work. There was almost no home where someone had not been taken away—the whole community was shrouded in mourning. People no longer cared for their own lives. The living envied the dead.

The Germans, alarmed at the sudden reduction of their work force, ordered everybody to report, but the order was met with total apathy. This was the first time that the Germans had met non-compliance. The Big Action had destroyed the illusion that work provides safety: The Ghetto and its leadership had been shaken into their terrible reality.

For this reason, Jordan and Rauca came to the Council to provide assurance, in the name of the German authorities, that the Big Action was the last, and no more Actions would take place. The Ghetto could enter a period of calm in which the Jews were expected to fulfill their quotas of work faithfully. This assurance was met by skepticism by the Council. But what German assurances could not achieve, hunger did.

There were only two ways of bringing food into the Ghetto, both potentially life-threatening. One was to join the work brigades and trade outside, and the other was to trade through the fence. Of these, trading across the fence was by far the most dangerous. Bribes worked sometimes, but rarely. Potatoes hidden in large pockets, sacks of bread stowed away, occasionally even a half pound of sugar, a piece of bacon bought at exorbitant cost from a peasant or family: This was what trading was about.

Yet, the clearest means of survival was work, preferably work in the Ghetto. Work meant food; and the extra rations, although meager, were extremely important. For every additional ounce of bread received on the ration card, less food from the outside would have to be brought in or traded for. Work in the Ghetto could serve people who were too weak to march five or six miles to work and still be able to stand the rigors of hard manual labor. The Council, therefore, decided to give the establishment of workshops the highest priority. If the Germans allowed such workshops to be developed, it would increase the work force of the Ghetto substantially. Moreover, if local German officials could enrich themselves through these workshops, they would be interested in preserving the Jewish work force for their own benefit.

Thus, when Jordan visited the Council, the Council presented their idea to him. They stressed that the Ghetto had many first-class tailors, shoemakers, hatmakers; they could repair torn uniforms, boots, or hats for the army. Jordan showed interest. His answer came sooner than anticipated. The German rulers quickly realized the potential bonanza: They gave the Council the green light.

The Council started preparations immediately. A building on Krisciukacio Street, a place where thousands of homeless Jews were housed before the Big Action, was assigned as a place for the workshops.

One of the first workshops to be established was one to prepare graphic displays, staffed by Mr. Mishell and two friends, whom he refers to in his book as Peter and Nolik (Ben Zion Smidt). Graphic displays were important for the Council to keep count, and to display statistics. Armbands, signifying various work assignments, were manufactured in response to need. More important, the graphics department was charged with printing various edicts and proclamations, as a means of disseminating information in the Ghetto.

In the middle of November 1941, the premises assigned to the workshops were cleared and renovated. By the beginning of January 1942, the workshops started, with a tailor, a shoemaker, a furrier, and a hatter. Their first assignment was to fix 5000 pieces of clothing— suits, coats, apparel robbed from Jews during an early-hours house-to-house search, and, later, from the various victims of the massacres. As soon as the workshops got into full swing, the Germans started to use them for mending the uniforms of their army.

In a report dated April 29, 1942, Mr. Michael Gemelizki[26] and his colleagues, Messrs. Brik, Kagan, Schwartz, and Friedman, reported on the fulfillment of the order given to them by the Council on December 5, 1941, to establish the Jewish community workshops in the home for the homeless. One of the early workshops to be established in 1942 was for *men's clothing*, operating with 12 sewing machines and other necessary equipment. On January 12, a *linen* sewing workshop and a *brushwork* workshop, employing 15 people, began operating. On January 21, 1942, a *shoemaking* workshop opened; on February 16, a *laundry* workshop and a *soap and candle manufacturing* workshop; on February 19, a *wool spinning* workshop; on March 9, a *sock-knitting* workshop; on March 10, a workshop for *children's toys* and a *tinker's* workshop; on March 18, a *saddler's* workshop; a workshop for *processing medical bandages* was also opened. Four hundred people were employed by the workshops by spring 1942; this number grew to 1800, working in shifts, in the coming months.

To grow food, around 300 women under the direction of the agronomist Shlomo Kelzon maintained some six acres of vegetable gardens. The work was supervised by Micha Mudrish. Under the initiative of Dr. Chaim Nachman Shapiro, eldest son of Chief Rabbi Shapiro, a youth movement named Eshel was established. Its members guarded the crops and ensured that they were picked and distributed fairly. Within the framework of this youth organization, young people were educated in Zionist and underground activities, while, at the same time, tending their gardens and thus feeding the Ghetto. The Germans favored the Jews having their own source of supply; it allowed them to take for themselves the meager rations allotted to the Ghetto. Allocation of the vegetables to inhabitants of the Ghetto was made from warehouses. Distribution throughout various parts of the Ghetto was carried out under the supervision of the supply department.

At about the same time, Mrs. Segal Varshavski, a leading Kovno kindergarten teacher (who was my teacher), and the wife of Dr. Elie Segal, head of the welfare department, established an *elementary school.* A clandestine kindergarten for orphaned and abandoned children was also set up. The Council also took tremendous pains in finding foster parents, who adopted orphaned children.

Ultimately, these workshops—the large workshops under the management of Moshe Segalson, and the small workshops under the management of Ephraim Bunim—proved vital elements in the Ghetto economy, and justified the Ghetto's existence to the Germans. They also secretly supplied Jewish partisans, who fled into the forests. For that reason, the Council insisted on managing the workshops directly, with no German interference.

And, in the jaws of death, institutions were created to maintain survival: as already mentioned, a *Police Force* to maintain order and carry out the instructions of

Figure 1 Elkhanan and Miriam Elkes, ca 1935

Figure 2 The young physician. Dr. Elkhanan Elkes, ca 1909

Figure 3 Physician in the Russian Army, ca 1916

Figure 4 Our house in Kaunas (Kestucio Street 6), 1934. The handwriting at the bottom is by the author's grandmother, the line at the side by the author's mother.

Figure 4a The Staff of the Jewish Hospital, "Bikur Cholim," Kovno, ca 1930.
Dr. Elkes is seated with Senior Colleagues, second row, ninth from right.
Note cobblestone paving of courtyard.

*Figure 5 Dr. Elkes with members of his Division of Internal Medicine,
Jewish Hospital (Bikur Cholim) Kovno, 1936*

Figure 6 Miriam and Sara Elkes, ca 1937

Figure 7 A family party, ca 1936. First from left Dr. Elkes, second from left Miriam Elkes, first from right the author

Figure 8 The house of the Ghetto Council.
Water color by Esther Lurie, 1943

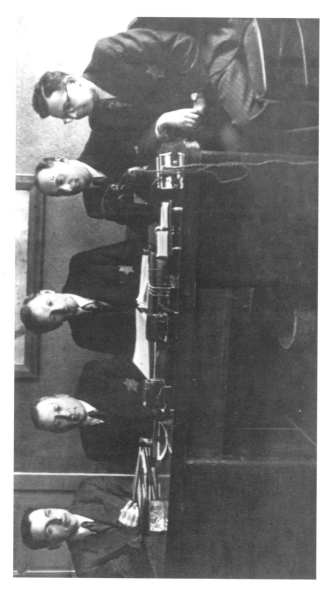

Figure 9 The Council. From left to right, Avraham Golub (Tory), Leib Garfunkel,
Dr. Elkes, Yakov Goldberg, Zvi Levin.
Archives of Avraham Tory, 1943

Figure 10 Dr. Elkes at his desk.
Archives of Avraham Tory, 1943

*Figure 11 On the job: Dr. Elkes and Dr. Berman.
Archives of Avraham Tory, 1943*

Figure 12 Dr. Moses Brauns (courtesy of Dr. Jack Brauns)

Figure 13 Esther Lurie-Shapiro, 1981

Figure 14 The wooden bridge connecting the "small Ghetto" to the "big Ghetto."
Esther Lurie, 1941

Figure 15 "Democracy Square": Site of roll call and selection before the "Big Action" of October 28, 1941. Water color, Esther Lurie, 1943

Figure 16 The road to the Ninth Fort.
Water color, Esther Lurie, 1943

Figure 17 Room after slaughter.
Pen and ink, Esther Lurie, 1941

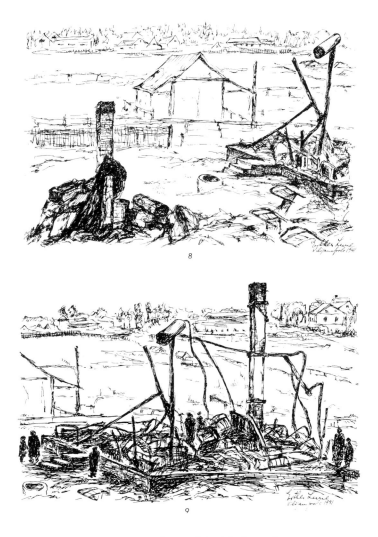

8

9

Figure 18 "What was left of the hospital."
Pen and ink, Esther Lurie, 1941

Figure 19 The Yellow Badge.
Pen and ink, Esther Lurie, 1941

Figure 20 Deportation to satellite labor camps. Fall 1943
Pen and ink, Esther Lurie, 1943

Figure 21 Deportation to satellite labor camps: Aleksotas and Sanciai.
Pen and ink, Esther Lurie, 1943

Figure 22 "Off to forced labor in the morning." Main gate.
Pen and ink, Esther Lurie, 1943

Figure 23 Deportation to satellite labor camps.
Pen and ink, Esther Lurie, 1943

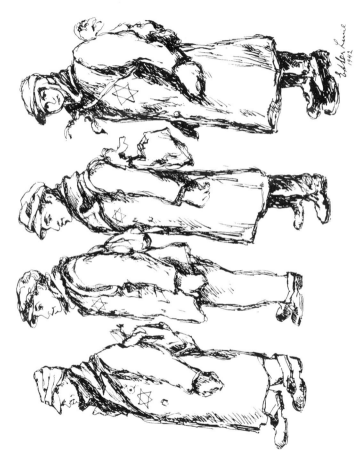

Figure 24 Four airfield workers
Pen and ink, Esther Lurie, 1942

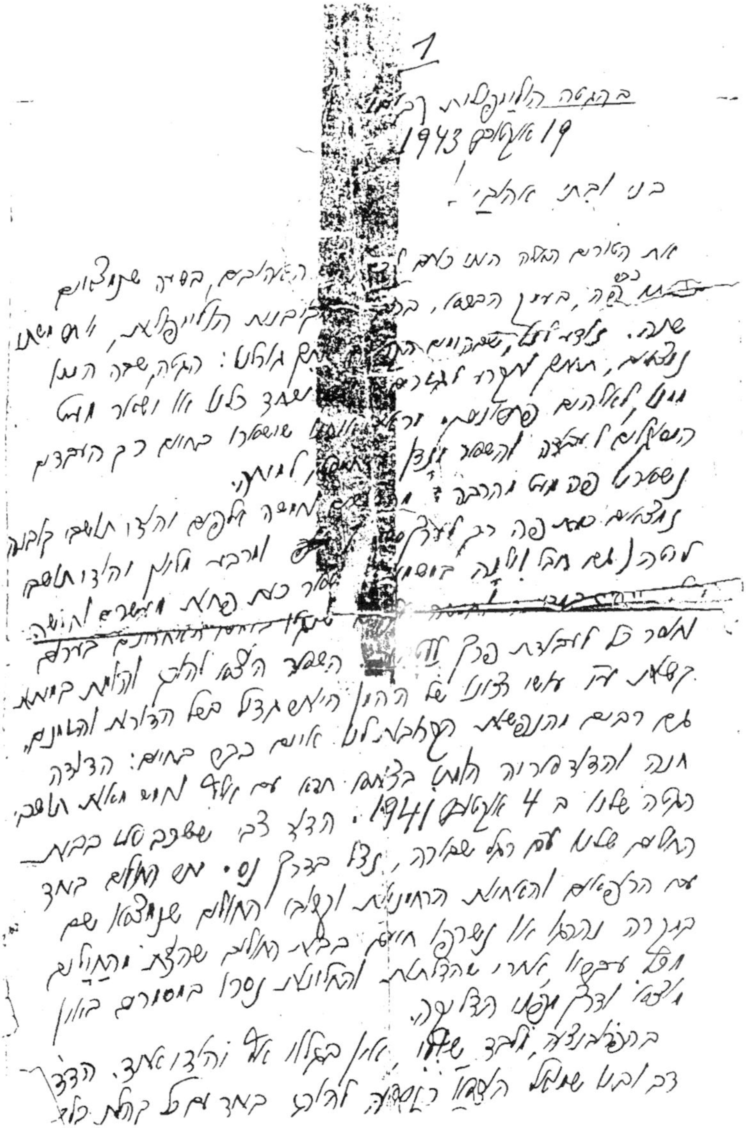

19 אוקטובר 1943

בני ובתי אהובי!

Figure 25 First page of letter of Dr. Elkhanan Elkes to the author and his sister Sara, October 19, 1943

68

*Figure 26 Dr. Elkhanan Elkes. Portrait executed in Ghetto.
Pen ank ink, Esther Lurie, 1943*

Figure 27 Dr. Elkhanan Elkes on his deathbed, Landsberg-Dachau, October 17, 1944. Artist unknown.

Figure 28 Entrance to the Jewish Cemetery near Landsberg.
Photo: Joel Elkes

Figure 29 Gravestone marking the
approximate resting place of
Dr. Elkhanan Elkes. Erected by Hans
Malbin, the author's uncle, in 1948.
Photo: Joel Elkes

Figure 30 Inscription on Gravestone.
It reads: "Here rests among his Brethren in
Sorrow our Dear Husband and Father
Dr. Elkhanan Elkes
Head ('Nassi') of the Community Kovno in
times of Peril and Mortal Danger."
(Translation into Hebrew by S. Goldsmith)
Photo: Joel Elkes

Figure 31 Hope: Miriam Elkes, Tel Aviv. Photo: Joel Elkes 1959

Figure 32 Hope: Tampa, 1983. From left to right, Avraham Tory, Lucy Elstein-Lavon and Joel Elkes. Photo: Sol Littman

Figure 33 Hope: Sara and Joel Elkes, Leicester, 1990. Photo: Josephine Rhodes

Figure 34 Hope: Avraham and Pnina Tory in their apartment in Tel Aviv, 1991.
Photo: Joel Elkes

Figure 35 Hope: Following the conferment of an honorary degree by the Hebrew
University, Jerusalem, upon the author. June 26, 1989. From left to right: Avraham
Tory, Joel Elkes, and Sara Elkes. Photo: Moshe Abeles

Figure 36 Remembrance: Inscription on memorial plaque affixed to Dr. Elkes's House (Kestucio 6/8) in Kovno on the 50th Anniversary of the destruction of the Kovno Ghetto. It reads in Lithuanian and Hebrew: "Here lived between the years 1930 and 1941, the Physician Dr. Elkhanan Elkes, Head of the Jewish Community Kovno, who died in 1944 in Concentration Camp Dachau"

the Council; a *Court,* under Prof. Beliatskin, to ensure the rule of law; a *Labor Office,* to register, direct, and protect all those working—in brigades outside the Ghetto as well as within its walls; a *Food Office* to ensure the equitable distribution of food either obtained from the Germans or produced within the Ghetto (this office was also charged with the distribution of firewood); a *Social Welfare Office* to distribute social benefits—foodstuffs, articles of clothing, money—upon proven evidence of need; and a *Health Office,* which administered the hospital and clinic and worked closely with both the social welfare office and the food office. Dr. Moshe Berman, internist, Dr. Benjamin Zacharin, surgeon, and Dr. Moses Brauns, specialist in infectious diseases, were the key physicians in the Ghetto.

The function of the Health Department can be illustrated by the management of an extremely serious typhus epidemic in the autumn of 1942. It was Dr. Brauns who brought this epidemic under control. The Germans had sustained enormous losses to typhus; the infection, carried by lice, broke out among Lithuanian workers tending the German wounded. The conditions in the Ghetto favored the development of infection—crowding, hunger, open cesspools, etc. News of infection in the Ghetto could have meant the instant destruction and burning of the Ghetto—just as the destruction of the Infectious Diseases Hospital on October 4, 1941, had signified the Germans' ruthless response to even the thought of contagious sickness among Jews.

A secret meeting, chaired by Dr. Elkes, was held. To his immense credit, Dr. Brauns undertook to control the infection. He did not report the existence of some known cases of typhus to the authorities. The disease was renamed "influenza," and Dr. Brauns—having obtained special allocations of food, soap, and nurses from the Council—treated 70 cases; only three died—an extraordinarily low mortality for the condition. Neither the Lithuanians nor the Germans learned what had transpired. A threat to the very life of the Ghetto had been averted.

There was also a *Housing Department*, which had the terrible task of re-allocating housing as, over the months and years, the space of the Ghetto was steadily curtailed and reduced. An *Office of Economic Affairs* controlled the payment of moneys or distribution of articles (until all money was taken away by the Germans). A *Department of Culture and Education* was in charge of both the kindergarten and the elementary/secondary schools, headed by Dr. Nachman Shapiro. A *Vocational School* under Dr. Jacob Oleiski was also established. Finally, a *Registration Office* was charged with issuing identity-registration cards to all—everyone without exception—who made a call on the institutions, and keeping track of the population statistics of the Ghetto. Later, however, registration cards were falsified or destroyed to ensure the safety of people in hiding.

Yet this thin crust of life was always floating on the lava below. Though it is hard to believe, even deep into

1942 the Council was unaware of the enormity of the death industry in places nearby. The single radio, belonging to the Zionist underground and hidden in the cellar of the pharmacy, gave German news: It did not tell what was happening to Jews elsewhere under German occupation.

It was a report by a non-Jew, Irena Adamovitch, on July 8, 1942, that brought home to the Council the enormous dimensions of the tragedy. Irena Adamovitch was a Polish Catholic woman, aged about 30, who had developed close relations with members of the Jewish resistance in Warsaw. In June and July 1942, she traveled from one Ghetto to another, passing information about life in the various communities. It was through her that the Jewish underground first learned of Ghettos in Poland, of Vilna, of Belsen, Sobibor, Majdanek, and Auschwitz; of gas chambers and crematoria; of resistance, and partisans in the Polish forests and labor camps—an encouragement for the partisans who were gathering in Lithuania. It was people like her—non-Jews—who encouraged members of the Ghetto to identify reliable non-Jews—both lay and clergy—to establish safe escape routes. There were renewed clandestine contacts. Sometimes they worked magnificently; at others, they proved cruel traps. Children were smuggled out, hidden in sacks, among bags of potatoes, to be handed over to clergy or friendly families. The great and valiant Reverend Bronius Paukstys[27] planned and brought about the escape of Pnina Tory, her daughter,

Shulamith, and later Tory himself, at the risk of his life—not once, but several times over. Chief Justice Aharon Barak—President of the Supreme Court of Israel, and an author of the Camp David Treaty—was smuggled out of the Kovno Ghetto and kept in hiding and safety outside. As recorded by Tory and others, Dr. Elkes and his Council encouraged these escapes by all means possible.

Joys: The Day and Beyond

When man is in pain or anguish, Goethe says somewhere, he sings. And so it was in the Ghetto. Though life could end any day, there were joys to share and to sustain. These joys had to be practiced in secret, and some in silence. There were observances of the Jewish New Year, of Yom Kippur and Passover: Tory's and Mishell's descriptions of these high and secret festivals—remnants of families celebrating what might be their last reunion—are poignant in the extreme.

The police force comprised some of the community's ablest musicians, star performers of the old symphony orchestra. So the Council passed off the symphony as the police band, and there were regular concerts of the clandestine symphony orchestra. There were dances; there were choirs. Poems and songs sprang up, fueled by anguish and despair, by defiance and hope. There was also a literature circle, which met in Pnina Sheinson's room every other week. Throughout, physical exercise was never forgotten, especially for the young. The police played a great educational role in the training of the youngsters, especially for future partisan work. Much of this was regularly reported to, and promoted by, the Council.

It should be stated that for nearly ten months in 1942, Dr. Elkes was ill, confined to bed or to a chair, and directed the affairs of the Council from his dwelling. On January 11, 1942, as Chairman of the Council, he had waited, on a cold and bitter night, at the main gate of the Ghetto to welcome 5000 Jews from Vienna and Germany who were to be accommodated in the Ghetto. They did not come but arrived later, to be taken straight to the Ninth Fort and killed. Dr. Elkes became severely ill with rheumatoid arthritis that week, and did not begin to recover for nearly a year.

On January 31, 1943, von Paulus surrendered at Stalingrad. The message was received and understood by victims and oppressors alike. Among the victims, whispers of hope and rumors of resistance by the underground competed with the stark foreboding of carnage carried out by a savaged enemy. Among the oppressors the deadly dialectic was resumed. There were those who favored work, and those who wished to proceed with the business of killing. In the short term, the work faction won a respite; in the long term, the SS prevailed, ruthlessly and absolutely.

The workshops represented an asset to their masters, not only in terms of sheer profit, which was huge, but in terms of job justification and physical safety. Warm offices instead of the frozen wastes of the Eastern Front. Productivity and supply for the German army, instead of fighting in uniform. There was a perceptible, but deceptive, change in attitude, played out against bizarre fluctuations among persons and events. Thus, for example, on February 19, 1943, the Kovno papers printed in full Goebbels' hate speech entitled, "Alarm! The West is in Danger," calling for the unconditional and total extermination of all Jews everywhere.

On February 22, a very apprehensive Tory meets Miller, the local Ghetto ruler, to find him surprisingly friendly.[28] The same day, Miller visits Dr. Elkes in the Council offices, his first visit after Dr. Elkes's illness. The conversation is polite, correct. Miller is even solicitous about Dr. Elkes's health, and suggests that Dr. Elkes increase the supply of medicines in the Ghetto, to avoid epidemics. At the end of the conversation Dr. Elkes thanks Miller for his visit, and Miller responds, "I do it willingly. It was my pleasure."

On February 25, Cramer, the head of the Kovno civil administration, arrives at the Council offices, in the company of three senior officials—"Top Beasts" (Hohe Tiere—in German), as they are called. They inspect the workshops and products and get an account of their manufacturing and destination. With clear pride, Cramer impresses his visitors that everyone in "his" Ghetto was working for the Reich.

Later the same day, Miller impresses upon Tory that he, Miller, is responsible for the Ghetto and is duty-bound to organize a large labor force to play its part. "You must sow fields," he tells Tory, "in such a way that every visitor will marvel at them." And six days after the Goebbels speech comes the following astonishing statement: "After the war, the Jews will be granted a piece of land, a territory of their own, where they will be able to live like other nations."[29] An unintended vision of Israel from a Nazi administrator in Kovno Ghetto?

There are consequences. Food supplies to the Ghetto increase—coffee, sugar, even diluted jam and artificial honey. But Tory has no illusions, nor has Dr. Elkes. "Everything we do," Tory writes on February 12,[30] "all things we go through, seem to us as a necessary evil, a temporary hardship, so that we may reach our goal and fulfill our duty to keep on going, to keep spinning the golden thread of the eternal glory of Israel, in order to prove to the world the will of our people to live, under any circumstances and situations. These goals supply us with the moral strength to preserve our lives, and to ensure the future of our people."

A later entry by Tory (of May 20, 1943)[31] conveys the counterpoint:

> You behold the Ghetto again, the Council build-ing, the inmates with yellow patches on their clothes, their brows furrowed with worry, their questioning eyes. You climb the stairs and feel the sharp gaze of the ordinary Ghetto inmates. They are curious to know, they read from the expression on your face what the day will bring, whether there's any news,

what has just happened, whether everything is still the way it was. They know that the Council members are short on words; they are responsible, sober-minded people who speak briefly and to the point. So the curious look into our faces. By chance, they will discover something from an expression, a look. It is common knowledge that the Council members know quite a lot, but they are not loquacious. They fill their mouths with water, like mutes. It is often said that the Council carries a heavy burden; that it faces constant danger; but only a few are aware of the exact nature of this burden and the danger. Even they, however, do not know everything; just a fragment, a hint. No one has any idea of the incidents, the experiences and the dangers, that members of the Council have gone through in this building. In all likelihood, only a few people will know about them in the future. Human speech is powerless to relate what has happened in this building in the past, each day, every hour, pregnant with danger.

As the weeks proceed, the Gestapo insists on their share of the action. On February 18, 1942, there is an Action to confiscate all printed matter and books; on May 1, the Ghetto boundaries are reduced: There are to be five such reductions in all. On August 26, all synagogues and schools are ordered closed. On November 18, a young man, Mek, who tried to escape, is executed by public hanging, following the arrest and subsequent release of Council members Garfunkel, Goldberg, and

Golub (Tory). On February 4, 1943, 50 Jews are murdered at random, as revenge and warning for the lost battle of Stalingrad. The Council is caught in the usual avalanche of orders, decrees, and countermands to throw it off balance.

In June 1943, Avraham Tory convenes a meeting of fellow students from his old fraternity. At that meeting, he reports for the first time, to a totally ignorant group, the extent of the carnage in Poland, and the liquidation of the Warsaw Ghetto. It is the first time that people in the Ghetto have heard of death vans, transports, the death factories of Auschwitz, Treblinka, and Majdanek. Avraham Tory concludes (I am paraphrasing from Mr. Mishell):[32]

> For the last month or so, our Ghetto Council has been wrangling with the problem of what to do. It considered revolt, in the manner of the Warsaw Ghetto. Under our conditions, however, this is totally impossible. First, Lithuanians are not ready to cooperate. Second, our Ghetto consists mainly of small wooden houses, and there is no way to barricade ourselves to launch even a semblance of a fight. We have therefore charted a different course whereby we are trying to get as many Jews as possible working for the Germans. Any German who profits from us will be interested in the status quo, and not in our extermination. Any delay and postponement of the Final Solution may ultimately bring us a discharge. As always it is our aim to save as many Jews as we can.

There are three ways of surviving. One is to join the underground and move into the forests. Anyone willing should join the partisans. The Council is doing everything possible to create a line, particularly into the forests of the Vilna area. We even have weapons.

Second is to find a Lithuanian who is a close enough friend and willing to take risks to save your life.

Finally, start building hiding places. The better the hiding place, the better the chance of survival. The war will not last forever. The Nazis will be brought to their knees. Hopefully, we can survive long enough to see it. So, again, hiding places right away.

The goal of this meeting is to drive you to action. This is my message to you today.

Thus, the period of the three options began. The clandestine radio brought good news. On July 22, the Russians mount their counteroffensive, demolishing the Nazis along the entire front. In the Ghetto fierce jealousies now begin among the Germans as to how to carry out the standing order for the destruction of all Jews. The administrators are unwilling to relinquish their work force, but the SS want to proceed with the killing. By the beginning of September the SS finally win. *Obersturmfuehrer* Wilhelm Goecke, known as a liquidator of Ghettos in Poland, is appointed ruler of Ghetto Kovno Viljampole.

9
K. Z. Kauen

Goecke's plan was simple. First, deprive the Ghetto of the protection of the Jewish Police; second, divide up the Ghetto and turn over security to the SS; third, move workers into concentration-camp-like encampments away from the main Ghetto; fourth, destroy women and children, and those in hiding; fifth, destroy the physical structure of the Ghetto; sixth, leave and retreat.

It is against this background that on September 29, the Jewish community celebrated Rosh Hashana. Yom Kippur fell on October 8. The Council cleared a room in the hospital for services; the police required that the service be conducted in silence. Tory addressed the audience.[33]

> History does not care what happens to the Jews. It has never recorded our torment, and will try conveniently to forget this most shameful period in human annals. . . . It is therefore that I admonish you: Do not give up. Try to survive. Hide. Escape the Ghetto. Go

to the forests. We must survive to tell this tale of horror to the comfortable world that does not want to hear us. . . . I want you all to understand that this is the last Yom Kippur in the Ghetto. There will be no more Ghetto by this time next year. It is everybody's responsibility to find a way to survive. The story must be told.

And so began the final phase of the Final Solution. The murder of the Jewish Police and the torture of some to reveal hiding places—during which the great Ika Greenberg died without revealing a thing; a terrible Action in Siauliai, killing 800 children; the deportation and killing of 2000 Jews in Estonia; the transformation, by November 1, of Ghetto Kaunas to Concentration Camp Kauen; a steady shrinking of the tiny living space, making the crowding virtually unbearable. There was also registration of all, upon pain of death, to provide accurate lists for death or deportation—the Council knowing full well that several thousand were in hiding, and not reporting their presence.

10

The Letter

On October 19, 1943, Dr. Elkes writes a letter to Sara and me. It is the only testament from a Council leader to survive the Holocaust. He entrusts the letter to Avraham Tory, who encloses it in the crate to be buried last. In November, Dr. Elkes requests the letter back, to add a postscript (dated November 11) telling us of the transformation of the Ghetto to Concentration Camp (K.Z.) Kauen. In January 1944, without warning or explanation, he hands the letter to Tory. On March 23, 1944, Avraham Tory is with Dr. Elkes and—as he put it—"his noble wife, Miriam," in their tiny room in the Ghetto. Also present is Advocate Garfunkel. Tory's escape is being discussed. Dr. Elkes is quite definite: "If you were my son," he says, "I would say to you, 'Go, go,' for who like you knows the darkest happenings of the Ghetto? Your mission is one of the greatest importance." That night Avraham Tory, disguised as a drover, escapes. Later he meets with Pnina, who carries my father's letter, protected in greaseproof paper, in her bra, "next to her heart," as she puts it. She is to carry it thus for many months. The letter reaches me in the autumn of 1945.

The text of this letter, written in magnificent Hebrew, follows.[34] Some personal passages have been omitted. It is dated October 19, 1943:

My beloved son and daughter,

I am writing these lines, my dear children, in the vale of tears of Viljampole, Kovno Ghetto, where we have been for over two years. We have now heard that in a few days our fate is to be sealed. The Ghetto is to be crushed and torn asunder. Whether we are all to perish, or whether a few of us are to survive, is in God's hands. We fear that only those capable of slave labor will live; the rest probably are sentenced to death.

We are left, a few out of many. Out of the 35,000 Jews of Kovno, approximately 17,000 remain; out of a quarter of a million Jews in Lithuania (including the Vilna district), only 25,000 live, plus 5000 who, during the last few days, were deported to hard labor in Latvia, stripped of all their belongings. The rest were put to death in terrible ways by the followers of the greatest Haman of all times and of all generations. Some of those dear and close to us, too, are no longer with us. Your Aunt Hannah and Uncle Arieh were killed with the 1500 souls of the Ghetto on October 4, 1941. Uncle Zvi (Hirsch), who was lying in the hospital suffering from a broken leg, was saved by a miracle. All the patients, doctors, nurses, relatives, and visitors who happened to be there were burned to death, after soldiers had blocked all the doors and windows of the hospital and set fire to it. In the provinces, apart from Siauliai, not a single Jew survives. Your Uncle Dov and his son Samuel were taken out and killed with the rest of the Kalvarija community during the first months of the war, that is—about two years ago.

Due to outer forces and inner circumstance, only our own Ghetto has managed to survive and live out its Diaspora life for the past two years, in slavery, hard labor, hunger, and deprivation. (Almost all our clothing, belongings, and books were taken from us by the authorities.)

The last massacre, when 10,000 victims were killed at one time, took place on October 28, 1941. Our total Community had to go through the "selection" by our rulers: life or death. I am the man who, with my own eyes, saw those about to die. I was there early on the morning of October 29, in the camp that led to the slaughter at the Ninth Fort. With my own ears I heard the awe-inspiring and terrible symphony, the weeping and screaming of 10,000 people, old and young—a scream that tore at the heart of heaven. No ear had heard such cries through the ages and the generations. With many of our martyrs, I challenged my Creator; and with them, from a heart torn in agony, I cried: "Who is like you in the Universe, my Lord!" In my effort to save people here and there, I was beaten by soldiers. Wounded and bleeding, I fainted, and was carried in the arms of friends to a place outside the camp. There, a small group of about 30 or 40 survived—witnesses to the fire.

We are, it appears, one of the staging centers in the East. Before our eyes, before the very windows of our houses, there have passed over the last two years many, many thousands of Jews from southern Germany and Vienna, to be taken, with their belongings, to the Ninth Fort, which is some kilometers from us. We learned later that they were killed—they were told they were coming to Kovno to settle in our Ghetto.

From the day of the Ghetto's founding, I stood at its head. Our community chose me, and the authorities confirmed me as a chairman of the Council of Elders, together with my friend, the advocate Leib Garfunkel, a former member of the Lithuanian parliament, and a few other close and good people concerned and caring for the fate of the surviving few. We are trying to steer our battered ship in furious seas, when waves of decrees and decisions threaten to drown it every day. Through my influence I succeeded, at times, in easing the verdict and in scattering some of the dark clouds that hung over our heads. I bore my duties with head high and an upright countenance. Never did I ask for pity; never did I doubt our rights. I argued our case with total confidence in the justice of our demands.

In these hardest moments of our life, you, my dear ones, are always before us. You are present in our deepest thoughts and in our hearts. In the darkest nights, your mother would sit beside me, and we would both dream of your life and your future. Our innermost desire is to see you again, to embrace you, and to tell you once again how close we are to you, and how our hearts beat as we remember you and see you before us. And is there any time, day or night, when your memory is not with us? As we stand here, at the very gates of hell, with a knife poised at our necks, only your images, dear ones, sustain us.

With regard to myself, I have little to report. Last year I suffered an acute and severe attack of rheumatoid arthritis, which kept me bedridden for nine months. However, even in the most difficult days of my illness, I carried on in my community, and from my bedside participated actively in the work of my friends. Now I am better; it has been about six months since I ceased being regarded as sick. I am not fully well, either, but I continue to work ceaselessly, without rest or respite.

About six months ago we received a message from Uncle Hans, transmitted to us by way of the Red Cross; it said that you were all right. The little note, written by a stranger, took nine months to reach us. We have written and written to you by way of the Red Cross and private persons. Have any of our words reached you? We are desolate that during our stay here we could not contact you and tell you that we are still among the living. We know full well how heavily the doubt of our survival weighs upon you, and what strength and confidence you would draw from the news that we are alive. This would certainly give you courage and belief in work and life with a firm and clear goal. I deeply fear despair, and the kind of apathy that tends to drive a person out of this world. I pray that this may not happen to you. I doubt, my beloved children, whether I will ever be able to see you again, to hug you and press you to my heart. Before I leave this world and you, my dear ones, I wish to tell you once again how dear you are to us, and how deeply our souls yearn for you.

Remember, both of you, what Amalek has done to us. Remember and never forget it all your days; and pass this memory as a sacred testament to future generations. The Germans killed, slaughtered, and murdered us in complete equanimity. I was there with them. I saw them when they sent thousands of people—men, women, children, infants—to their death, while enjoying their breakfast, and while mocking our martyrs. I saw them coming back from their murderous missions—dirty, stained from head to foot with the blood of our dear ones. There they sat at their table—eating, drinking, listening to light music. They are professional executioners.

The soil of Lithuania is soaked with our blood, killed at the hands of the Lithuanians themselves;

Lithuanians, with whom we have lived for hundreds of years, and whom, with all our strength, we helped to achieve their own national independence. Seven thousand of our brothers and sisters were killed by Lithuanians in terrible and barbarous ways during the last days of June 1941. They themselves, and no others, executed whole congregations, following German orders. They searched—with special pleasure—cellars and wells, fields and forests, for those in hiding, and turned them over to the "authorities." Never have anything to do with them; they and their children are accursed forever.

I am writing this at an hour when many desperate souls—widows and orphans, threadbare and hungry—are camping on my doorstep, imploring us for help. My strength is ebbing. There is a desert inside me. My soul is scorched. I am naked and empty. There are no words in my mouth. But you, my most dearly beloved, will know what I wanted to say to you at this hour.

And now, for a moment, I close my eyes and see you both standing before me. I embrace and kiss you both; and I say to you again that, until my last breath,

I remain your loving father,

Elkhanan

November 11, 1943

P.S. I add a few lines. It has been two weeks now since we passed from one authority to another. They have now changed our name; instead of being "the Ghetto," we are called "Concentration Camp No. 4, Kovno," with new officials and functionaries. Our share of misery is not over yet. On the 26th of last month they took 2709 people out of our Ghetto. According to information we have received, they separated the children and the elderly—they are probably dead by now. Those who were able to work were sent to Estonia to hard labor. On the 5th of this month they took out of Siauliai all the children under 13, as well as the elderly men and women. They were told that they were being brought to Kovno. They are probably all dead now.

As to our fate, we await it in the very near future. These lines, together with some documents, I am putting in a safe place. I pray that they may reach your hands one day.

With love, affection, and my blessing,

Your father

P.S. We have learned from a reliable source that the Germans are trying to erase any trace of their murders. The bones of our martyrs are to be burned in the Ninth Fort and in other places, by people who are experts in this kind of job (chemists).

11

Landsberg-Dachau

By the beginning of 1944, the "Final Solution" was escalating rapidly. On March 25–26, a terrible Action against children and the sick takes place in the Ghetto. Houses are set on fire and dogs are used to hunt out the infirm. Two thousand children and sick are killed. On April 4, the Council is arrested. Some members are tortured to reveal hiding places. On July 6, Goecke informs Dr. Elkes that the Ghetto will cease to exist and will be evacuated to Germany.

To the last, Dr. Elkes argues with Goecke that it is to his advantage to leave the Ghetto alone. But the march of events is now inevitable.

And thus, on July 13 Dr. Elkes leads the first group of his congregation to the railway station. He has extracted a promise from Goecke that men and women, and especially families, would not be separated. At the station, as they force their human fodder into cattle trucks, the guards know nothing of such promises. Dr. Elkes tries to intervene. Seizing an officer by his lapels,

he cries out, "You promised me, you are a German officer, you have given me your word"; he is brutally beaten
and bundled into the cattle truck.

The train is destined for Kaufering-Landsberg-
Dachau, but goes by way of Tiegenhof. My mother, her
sister Trude, and Lucy Elstein are separated from my
father and sent to Stutthof, near Danzig. Dr. Elkes and
his fellow prisoners arrive in Landsberg, at Camp I, on
or around July 15. Here the awesome misery over-
whelms him; he is assigned to the infirmary, where he
gives himself without stint. I have it from eyewitnesses.

His brother, Hirsch (Zvi), was with him. In a letter to
me dated September 18, 1945, he writes,

What your father had to suffer here, physically
and mentally, is impossible to describe. Yet, he carried
all with immense dignity. "These people can never
humiliate me," he used to say, referring to his guards.

The bitterness of our life here only served to bring
the sorrows of others closer to his heart. He knew no
rest. The fire he put into everything he undertook was
not quenched; on the contrary, it was to consume him,
in the end.

You know that his physical constitution was
never the strongest, and that his tireless spirit did not
have a worthy servant in his fragile body. Yet he
would not hear of taking care of himself. Even here,
no work, no service, no abuse even of his kindness,
was ever refused; and by serving others, he consumed

himself. Thanks to his energy, he managed, for a time, to hold his equilibrium, but his strength continued to ebb; and, with the deepest anguish, we saw things worsen without being able to help. His will to live, too, ebbed. He awaited death as a merciful release from his spiritual anguish. "Such a life is unseemly; I cannot watch this suffering; I must be away" ("Ich muss weg"). He lay on his hard bunk, very quiet, looking into the distance, accepting fate, in unspeakable pain. He lay there for 14 days, a few teaspoonfuls of water his only nourishment. He remained conscious until his last breath, and, on the 17th of October, 1944, at 4:15 A.M., he had done.

"Not an eye remained dry as the news of Dr. Elkes's death spread throughout the camps," reported my uncle.

He was buried in a separate grave, distinct from the mass grave into which bodies were usually consigned. Thirty days after his death—the Jewish *Shloshim* (Hebrew for "thirty")—a small band of about 30 or 40 inmates gathered secretly in the dark to conduct a memorial service. Dr. Gringauz delivered the eulogy—in a low voice, lest he be overheard by the guards. A drawing (figure 27) by an unknown artist shows him on his deathbed. A stone erected with the help of my uncle (my mother's brother), Hans Malbin, marks his approximate resting place. The inscription (in Hebrew) reads in translation:

Here rests among his Brethren in Sorrow our
Beloved Husband and Father Dr. Elkhanan Elkes.
Leader ("Nassi") of Community Kovno in times of
Anguish and Mortal Danger.

Even my sister Sara and I, however, did not know the
full meaning of Dr. Elkes's death until many years later.
In testimony dated May 26, 1996,[35] Mr. Moissej
Aronson, of Raanana, Israel, who had shared the camp
hut in which Dr. Elkes had died, states that Dr. Elkes's
refusal to take nourishment was an act of deliberate
protest. Apparently, the commandant, an SS Sergeant
Daum, ordered Dr. Elkes to use his influence with fellow
prisoners to "work more diligently" in the subterranean
factory that they were building, and encouraged him by
all kinds of inducements. The prisoners were on starva-
tion rations. Dr. Elkes "stated that his conscience would
not allow him to do this" and declared that unless the
terrible work conditions were improved and rations
increased (several prisoners were dying every day) he
himself would refuse food. Dr. Elkes, thus, went on a
hunger strike in Dachau.

My mother, who was separated from him just south
of Danzig, was sent with her sister, Trude Itzigsohn, and
Lucy Elstein to the notorious extermination camp of
Stutthof. After surviving a Death March, in which thousands perished, she and others were taken out on a ship
to be drowned in the North Sea. An RAF fighter patrol
spotted the boat, set it on fire, and forced it back to port

in Kiel. There on May 2, 1945, the captives were told
that they were free. The great Captain von Moltke saw
to their needs. My mother was taken to a hospital. A
British army surgeon wrote to me, at St. Mary's
Hospital, London, that he had my mother under his care.
I had to inform her of her husband's death.

She recovered in St. Ottilien Monastery, near Munich
in Bavaria, being helped in great measure by her brother
Hans Malbin who was with the United Nations Relief
and Recovery Administration at the time. She then
joined me for a time in England, and finally moved with
Sara to Israel, where she died on December 5, 1965.

She told me that, apart from the hope of seeing her
husband and us, two objects sustained her in captivity.
One was a piece of bread, which she always hid about
her person; the other was a broken piece of comb. She
kept the bread in case someone needed it more than she;
and no matter what, morning and night, she would
comb her hair to affirm her person.

12
Conversations

In February 1959 *Commentary* published a letter by Samuel Gringauz,[36] a colleague from the Ghetto. The letter was headed "Hero of Kovno" and argued that "it behooved us, above all, to preserve for generations noble images of men like Elkes." Had my father been alive to read this letter, he would, I feel sure, have noted it with an embarrassed smile, and proceeded with the immediate business of the day. Praise and power did not sit well with Elkhanan Elkes.

Yet, more than 50 years after his death, the memory of Dr. Elkes is still fresh in the minds of some. Again and again, strangers stop Sara or me when our name is mentioned and share with us some aspect of their lives that was touched by Dr. Elkes. I remember, for instance, being introduced to a guest at a party in Israel. We had chatted for a while, he not knowing who I was. Then he learned my name from someone who joined us. "Elkes?" he said— "Are you related to Dr. Elkhanan Elkes?" "Yes," I said, "I'm his son." At that point, the face of this very calm,

well-groomed, and cultivated man contorted; tears burst
forth, and within seconds he was sobbing, gripping me
in a helpless embrace. When he had composed himself
before his astonished friends, he could only stammer, "If
only you knew what influence your father's example has
had on my life." Then he gave an instance of what he
meant. "Someone I know," he said, "was in Dr. Elkes's
office—he was seeing him on business. Suddenly, a
Sturmfuehrer burst in to make demands of Dr. Elkes. He
put his jackboot on your father's chair. To this day, I cannot believe what happened next; for, calmly, Dr. Elkes
turned to the man and politely asked him to move his
boot, offering him, at the same time, with cold good
manners, a chair of his own. 'And now, what can I do for
you?' asked Dr. Elkes of the SS man; and then proceeded
with business."

A letter received quite recently by my sister Sara
speaks to Dr. Elkes's resourcefulness in time of danger.
The author is Mrs. Ilana Ash, daughter of Dr. Elkes's
Chief Nurse. Mrs. Ash now lives in London. The letter is
dated April 12, 1999. My sister did not know of Mrs.
Ash's existence until receiving the letter.

An extract follows:

A few months ago I received a remarkable gift
from my brother-in-law who lives in Israel—a book
entitled *Hidden History of the Kovno Ghetto*.[42] I was
born in this Ghetto. Looking through the book I
immediately found a few familiar names. I came
across the name and picture of Dr. Elkes. I will not

describe to you my emotions. My mother, who was a nurse, used to work with Dr. Elkes in the Jewish hospital before the war and remained his close friend throughout the hell of the ghetto. I was born on March 1942 in the Kovno Ghetto. Dr. Elkes delivered me and insisted that I be called Ilana—the Hebrew name of a tree, telling my mother that the new branches survive once the old tree is dead.

During the first Children's Action, when I was still a tiny baby, Dr. Elkes, your father, gave me a sleeping pill, helped my mother to put me in a linen bag. My mother—pretending that she just came back from town with a bag of potatoes (at this time they were still allowed to exchange clothes for food)—had to go to the square to witness executions.

My mom survived the Ghetto and Stutthof concentration camp (she died of cancer in 1967 in Vilnius). She smuggled me out of the Ghetto and I was saved by a Lithuanian family. My mother, like most of the survivors, as I learned later in my life, very seldom talked about the Ghetto. However, so often she would mention two names: Dr. Elkes and Dr. Abrasha Zilberg. I still remember sparks in her eyes when she mentioned these names. . . . The thoughts of your father are always with me—in my name, in my mom's stories, in the memory of my mom.

Many of Dr. Elkes's conversations are recorded by witnesses: They bear out his extraordinary reserve and presence of mind when facing his enemy. A few instances will serve.

In the entry of May 11, 1943,[37] Tory reports on an extraordinary clandestine meeting between a German officer and Dr. Elkes. The ultimate intention is to bring about a meeting between Dr. Elkes and Major General Heinz Jost, the feared Governor-General of Lithuania. As an intermediate step towards this contact, a meeting is to be arranged between Dr. Elkes and the German judge Lukas whom, as a then lawyer, Dr. Elkes had known before the war. Another contact from the olden days, Dr. Schtrauch (whom I remember as head of the German high school), is to be brought into the picture at a later date.

A number of meeting venues are discussed and dismissed, and a surprising one is arrived at. Lukas suggests a meeting at his own apartment. There are two reasons for this choice. First, the apartment is opposite the building of the city health department; in case of need, it could be argued that Dr. Elkes entered the apartment by mistake. Second, Lukas argues that no one would suspect a German judge of inviting a Jew into his home. For additional cover, the manager of the Ghetto pharmacy and Avraham Tory would accompany Dr. Elkes, but leave him alone to proceed to Judge Lukas's apartment.

In his entry Tory relates the account given him by Dr. Elkes:

> It was lunchtime. The table was set for Dr. Elkes
> also. Lukas greeted him warmly, and asked him to sit
> at the table. Dr. Elkes was seated in front of a large

mirror that gave him an opportunity to observe a unique spectacle: Lukas, a judge of the German court in Kovno, dressed in the Nazi uniform, swastika on his sleeve, sat at the table opposite the Jew Dr. Elkes, who was wearing yellow badges on his clothes, on the front and back.

He proceeds:

Lukas filled two glasses with wine, and raised his glass in a toast—"To better times." Dr. Elkes raised his glass, too, but could not bring himself to repeat his host's toast, contenting himself with a more modest response, "To the well-being and happiness of this household." The mirror reflected this rare scene, which inscribed itself indelibly on Dr. Elkes's mind.

As for the meeting with General Jost, nothing came of it despite the goodwill of Judge Lukas and Dr. Schtrauch.

In the entry for June 9, 1943,[38] Tory reports a meeting between Dr. Elkes, SS Master Sergeant Schtitz and Colonel Karl Jaeger—both ruthless and proven killers. The overt reason is to discuss rumors concerning further Actions in the Ghetto, which "interfere with the flow of work." The covert and real reason is to save two lives, those of Drs. Nabriski and Voschin, two physicians who had escaped from the Ghetto, had been sheltered by Lithuanians, and had been caught by the Gestapo. What follows is a condensed account of what transpired.

Jaeger receives Dr. Elkes and offers him a chair; Schtitz stands to attention. "What brings you here?"

asks Jaeger. "The fate of the Ghetto," says Dr. Elkes. "There are rumors of Actions." "Totally groundless," replies Jaeger. "We like to see people working. We only prosecute those engaged in sabotage or politics against us—Jew or Lithuanian." There is some more talk. As the meeting is on the point of breaking up, Dr. Elkes addresses the colonel again. 'There is another issue I wish to bring up. It concerns Dr. Nabriski and Dr. Voschin. Dr. Nabriski is a talented physician whose services as a gynecologist are of great importance to our hospital. His presence will ensure that women will not be absent for long periods after an abortion," Dr. Elkes continues. He has known Dr. Nabriski for ten years; he is an honest man and a fine physician. Jaeger does not let Dr. Elkes finish the sentence. "Let him go," he says, turning to Schtitz. "As ordered," says Schtitz. Dr. Elkes continues, "Dr. Voschin is a young colleague of mine. I can vouch for him." Again, Jaeger does not let him finish the sentence, but barks out the order, "Let Dr. Voschin go."

At this point, Dr. Elkes takes up the fate of the Lithuanians. "I would also like to mention the people who have given shelter to the physicians. I am speaking to you as one human being to another. These people acted out of humane and generous impulse. They received no material reward for sheltering these two physicians. Just as a judge would take into account whether a defendant acted out of malice or greed, or out of a human impulse, so I am asking you to weigh the motivation of these people before making a decision."

"Let the Lithuanians go," says Jaeger to Schtitz.

In the hallway, the Lithuanians cross themselves and try to kiss Dr. Elkes's hands. Embarrassed, he hurries on.

This visit has a sequel. On July 16,[39] Schtitz askes Dr. Elkes to see him as a patient. Such a visit—of an Aryan to a Jewish physician—is punishable by incarceration, and even death. The visit, therefore, takes place in secret. Dr. Elkes examines him and prescribes medication. "Do you sleep?" asks Dr. Elkes. "Yes," says Schtitz. "Do you dream?" asks Dr. Elkes. "No," says Schtitz. Afterwards Dr. Elkes tells Tory, "This patient, whom destiny has forced me to check, is shocking in the extreme. Just to touch him—whose hands are covered with the blood of Jews—was horrible. . . . Yet I suppose I did what I was meant to do. It may help to save lives."

On May 19, 1942, Dr. Alfred Rosenberg, Minister for Eastern Affairs, with a high entourage that includes Cramer, the German city governor of Kovno, visits the workshops.[40] At that meeting, Dr. Elkes pleads for increased rations to preserve the strength and productivity of the workers. The calm pathos of his plea, delivered in perfect German, takes the visitors by surprise. He is listened to without interruption at first. Then someone interjects: "How dare you talk to us as if you were our equal? You are just a dirty Jew, like the rest of you in the Ghetto."

"Quite so," says Dr. Elkes, "I am a Jew like the others, and that means very much. I belong to an ancient nation, which has experienced many decrees and much suffering through the ages. However, we always knew how to overcome oppression and slavery, which have come and gone in the waves of the centuries of our existence. There is no doubt in my mind that, in this war, too, we will overcome our suffering, so as to preserve the image of God—the same God who created you and created us."

Stadtkommissar Cramer's face is boiling as he listens. He storms out the door, leaving the other dignitaries standing.

On July 6, 1944, Dr. Elkes visits SS *Obersturmfuehrer* Wilhelm Goecke. The preceding months have seen terrible Actions, including the Children's Action. The end is near. I am paraphrasing my mother's account of that conversation.

"I am old," Dr. Elkes begins. "I have no fear of death; you can kill me on the spot. However, I have this to say to you. You listen to the radio, and we listen to the radio. You and I know that Germany has lost the war. No miracles can help you. Your patriotism cannot serve your fatherland or your party—certainly not by murdering thousands of Jews. But you can alleviate your conscience if you leave us alone. Don't supply trains for our evacuation. Postpone it until the Russians arrive. Take for yourself all the gold and valuables we still have. Leave us to be responsible for our own future. We are an ancient people with long memories and remember decency in times of peril." Dr. Elkes continues: "Whatever your answer, we will not forget."

Goecke is taken by surprise, and listens to the end. Then, drawing himself up, he gives his reply. "I am a

German officer, and I have my orders. I cannot postpone the evacuation. I assure you, you are not being sent to die." A relative truth, of course: The trains are meant for Stutthof and Dachau (a so-called "Work camp").

Dr. Elkes led his people to the trains on July 13. My mother reports that he walked firmly and erect.

13
Closing

I have told you a tale of life and death of a small community—a tiny statistic in the immensity of the
Holocaust and the unimaginable tragedies with which
our murderous century abounds. You and I will ask the
same question. How is it that it survived for so long—
long after other communities had been extinguished?
Was there any quality to the leadership that prolonged
survival? Or was it a freak of fate, a statistical play of the
law of averages?

I suggest to you that the leadership contributed decisively to its survival as an organized community, and that
the personal qualities of Dr. Elkes contributed decisively
to the leadership.

Put simply, Dr. Elkes *dared,* and dared from an inner
and unshakable conviction. As he wrote in his last letter—the only letter, I would remind you again, from a
Ghetto leader to his children to emerge from the
Holocaust—"Our community chose me. . . . I bore my
duties with head high and an upright countenance.

Never did I ask for pity; never did I doubt our rights. I argued our case with total confidence in the justice of our demands."

"Total confidence in the justice of our demands." I have tried to project myself into the awesome loneliness of that leadership, and the extraordinary qualities it took to maintain it. Imagine—while still naive in the ways of the SS—learning of the fate of the 534 intellectuals on the morning following the killing—and *lead;* of learning of the Action of October 4, 1941, which killed 1500, including his beloved sister and brother—and *lead;* of recovering from being beaten unconscious on the day of the Action that killed 9200—and resume leadership; being in bed for months on end, racked by severe pain— and *lead;* seeing through double agents, black marketeers, covetousness, jealousy, false accusation—and *lead;* and week in, week out, facing the lying, deceiving, conniving, deadly enemy—while shouldering the full responsibility for such confrontation—and continue to *lead.* How many times, I ask myself, must he have cried out for relief from his most awesome of responsibilities: The capsule of cyanide was always in his pocket. Yet, because he regarded his life as expendable, he could also use it as an asset in his dealing with the enemy. Somehow, he managed to walk through the barriers of fear to an extraordinary personal freedom.

In her searching Yarnton Trust Lecture,[41] Dr. Elizabeth Maxwell asks the question, "Why should the Holocaust be remembered and, therefore, taught?" It is

not a rhetorical question. Revisionism and trivialization
are afoot. The uniqueness and specificity of the event are
being obscured by huge historical shifts that assault us
week by week and tax to the utmost our capacity to
comprehend and exercise informed judgment. Among
today's fires, yesterday's fires appear less relevant. Yet no
one—not even the most arrogant of intellectuals—will
deny the crisis of the spirit that is abroad, irrespective of
continent or nation, affluence or destitution. People,
ordinary people—"We the People," as we say in
America—are looking for Meaning, derived not from
without, but from within.

So the story of the Holocaust must be taught, not
only as a stark and terrible warning for our dangerous
times, but as an affirmation of our Humanity, and of
Hope. I submit that I have told you a tale of Hope. For
a community to persist and endure—*as a community*—
in the face of the conditions that prevailed in Kovno
Ghetto, sends a message that goes to that place in the
heart where Meaning and Hope are conjoined. Hope is
not disembodied. Values and Belief are the sinews and
substance of Hope. There is a message for our times here,
short and direct: *"Hold on,"* it says, *"it is possible."*

These qualities never left Dr. Elkhanan Elkes; for to
him, the heart of the Jewish Ethic was the universal Ethic
of Man—the *Menschlichkeit*—of which he talked to
Sara and me in our youth. I see a direct line between the
Jewish officer in the Russian army who would not toler-
ate antisemitic talk in his presence, to the physician who

talked of Judaism to the German and Russian ambassadors, or counseled, comforted, and sustained an anguished Prime Minister, or confronted professional killers like Jaeger or Goecke in the hour of mortal danger to his community. He never was in doubt about his values, and never for one moment lost his belief in his people. Put simply, Dr. Elkes knew who he was.

Postscript

Some fifty-five years later, in the twilight of our murderous century, we search our former enemy's face. "How was it possible?" we ask. "Will it happen again?" And above all, "Do you truly understand why Justice is important and why it must be practiced, and must prevail?"

Eye meets eye, and, haltingly, hand gropes for hand. We both know our inner Truth. Yes, we must try and walk together. It will be a long walk.

Notes and References

Notes

1. Leib Garfunkel, *Kovnah Hayehudit Bekhurbana* [(in Hebrew:) The Destruction of Kovno's Jewry] (Jerusalem: Yad Vashem Publications, 1959), 47–48.
2. Avraham Tory, *Surviving the Holocaust: The Kovno Ghetto Diary* (Cambridge, Massachusetts, and London: Harvard University Press, 1990), 553 pp.
3. W.W. Mishell, *Kaddish for Kovno: Life and Death in a Lithuanian Ghetto* (Chicago: Chicago Review Press, 1988), 398 pp.
4. Sol Littman, *War Criminal on Trial: The Rauca Case* (Toronto: Lester and Orpen Dennys, 1983), 194 pp.
5. Garfunkel, *Kovnah Hayehudit Bekhurbana*, 330 pp.
6. Ephraim Oshry, *Khurban Litta* [(in Hebrew:) The Ruins of Lithuania, A Chronicle of the Destruction of the Sacred Jewish Communities of Lithuania] (New York and Montreal: Rabbi Oshry Book Committee, 1951), 468 pp.
7. Kovno, at that time the capital of a Russian province *(gubernija),* was destined to emerge later as Kaunas, the capital of the new Lithuanian Republic.
8. Esther Lurie, *A Living Witness: Scenes and Types* (Tel Aviv: Dvir Publishing Co., 1956), 19 pp. and 30 plates.
9. Before the War Avraham Tory was elected member of the Central Zionist Committee of Lithuania, and led the Maccabi team in Lithuania at the first Maccabiah Games in Palestine

in 1932. After the Liberation he continued to occupy a leading position with the Maccabi movement, serving between 1948 and 1968 on the Maccabi Executive and as its Honorary Secretary. He is one of the founders of the Maccabiah village (the Jewish Olympic Village) and serves as one its directors to this day. He is a member of the Presidium of the International Association of Jewish lawyers.

As a principal witness, he gave crucial testimony at the trials of three major war criminals:

H. Rauca—Head of the Jewish Desk of the Gestapo, Kovno; in Toronto, June 17, 1983

H. Schmitz—of the Gestapo, Kovno; in Wiesbaden, November 22–23, 1962

K. Palciauskas—Mayor of Kovno; in Tampa, March 1983

10. Tory, *Surviving the Holocaust,* xxii–xxiii.
11. Avraham Tory, *Ghetto Yom Yom* [(in Hebrew) Ghetto Day by Day] (Tel Aviv: Mossad Bialik, University of Tel Aviv, 1988), 608 pp.
12. Tory, *Surviving the Holocaust,* 3.
13. *Ibid.,* 6.
14. Littman, *The Rauca Case,* 43–62.
15. Tory, *Surviving the Holocaust,* 27.
16. Haman, killer of Jews. See the Book of Esther, Bible, Old Testament.
17. Tory, *Surviving the Holocaust,* 27.
18. *Ibid.,* 29.
19. Mishell, *Kaddish for Kovno,* 48–54.
20. There were two hospitals in the Ghetto—the Infectious Diseases Hospital and the General Hospital. The latter comprised the Departments of Medicine, Surgery, and Gynecology; the Orphanage; and the Old Age Home. On the morning of December 4, Dr. Moses Brauns, Dr. Zacharin and Jack Brauns (Dr. Brauns's son, who was working as a clerk in the hospital) were on their way to the hospital. They found the entry to the small Ghetto barred. The bridge leading from the big to the small Ghetto, was manned by armed guards. This circumstance saved their lives. The children from the Orphanage, the patients from the General hospital, and the inhabitants of the Old Age Home were subsequently taken to

the Ninth Fort and killed. My Uncle Hirsch, who was a patient at the hospital, survived by a freak event. He was discharged before that Action.

21. Tory, *Surviving the Holocaust*, 43–58.
22. Littman, *The Rauca Case*, 74–82.
23. Tory, *Surviving the Holocaust*, 49.
24. *Ibid.*, 53.
25. The lecture on which this Memoir is based was delivered on October 31, 1991, within two days of the fiftieth anniversary of the Great Action.
26. Tory, *Surviving the Holocaust*, 81.
27. A tree in honor of the Rev. Paukstys is planted in the Avenue of Righteous Gentiles at Yad Vashem, Jerusalem, Israel.
28. Tory, *Surviving the Holocaust*, 232–33.
29. *Ibid.*, 241.
30. *Ibid.*, 210.
31. *Ibid.*, 333.
32. Mishell, *Kaddish for Kovno*, 157.
33. *Ibid.*, 166.
34. Tory, *Surviving the Holocaust*, 503–07.
35. Moissej Aronson, Letter and Testimony dated May 26, 1996, to the U.S. Holocaust Museum, Washington, D.C.
36. Samuel Gringauz, "Hero of Kovno: Letter to the Editor" (*Commentary*, February 1959).
37. Tory, *Surviving the Holocaust*, 326–27.
38. *Ibid.*, 383–86.
39. *Ibid.*, 425–26.
40. Avraham Tory, reported in a personal communication, *"Hohe Tiere"* ["High Beasts"], 1987.
41. Elizabeth Maxwell, *Silence and Speaking Out* (Southampton, UK: University of Southampton, 1990), 27 pp.
42. *The Hidden History of the Kovno Ghetto*, Edited by Dennis B. Klein, U.S. Holocaust Museum (New York: Bullfinch Press, 1997) 255 pp.

Index

Actions 14, 34, 38, 40, 82, 95, 107, 110
Adamovitch, Irena 76
Aronson, Moissej 98
Ash, Ilana 101–102
Auschwitz 76, 83
Avodath Kodesh 11

Barak, Aharon 77
Beliatskin, Prof. Simon 10, 28, 74
Belsen 76
Berman, Dr. Moshe 4, 74
Bernstein, Israel 25
Block C 12
Bobelis, Governor 20
Brauns, Dr. Jack 4, 14, 31
Brauns, Dr. Moses 14, 31, 74–75
Bunim, Ephraim 44

Carnage 14, 15–20, 38
  in Poland 83
  concentration 17
Central Jewish Bank 21
Concentration Camp Kauen 85–86, 94
Council, Ghetto 2, 7, 20, 25–31, 81, 90, 95
Cramer, Hans 27–29, 80, 106–107

Dachau 96, 98, 108
Dauksos Street 21
Daum, SS Sergeant 98
Davidowitz, Dr. 30
Democracy Square 32–33, 36
destruction (of habitat) 17, 85
diary of Avraham Tory 9–14
Diaspora 89
Dizengoff Award 8–9

Einsatzkommando 16
Elkes, Dr. Elkhanan 1–6
  death 97–98
  early life 3–6
  election as *Oberjude* 22–24
  Hero of Kovno 100–108
  leadership 109–112
  testament and last letter 12, 88–94
Elkes, Dr. Hirsch 31, 88, 96
Elkes, Israel Meir 3
Elkes, Miriam 3, 6–7, 87, 98
Elkes, Sara 1, 7, 8, 87, 99, 111
Elstein-Lavon, Lucy 3, 7–8, 20, 96, 98
escape routes 75–76
Eshel youth movement 43
Estonia 86, 94

evacuation secretariat 20
extermination 17
Final Solution 2, 17, 27, 83, 86, 95
Fourth Fort 28–29
Garfunkel, Dr. Leib 2, 11, 17, 25, 35, 82, 87, 90
Gemelizki, Michael 43
German occupation: Lithuania 15–20
Gestapo 7, 18, 22, 28, 32, 82, 104
Ghetto 18–20
  organization 25–31, 44, 74–75
  synagogue 31
Ghetto Court 28, 74
Gilbert, Sir Martin 2, 11, 14
Goebbels 80–81
Goecke, Wilhelm 84, 95, 107–108 112
Goldberg, Jacob 17, 25, 35, 82
Goldschmidt, Shraga 12–13
Golub, Avraham 20, 25
Greenberg, Ika 86
Gringauz, Dr. Samuel 97, 100
Gymnassion Ivry Kovno 5

Ha Tiqua 24
Haman 21, 88
Head Jew (see Oberjude)
Health Department 74
Hebrew Gymnasium 5
Hebrew University, Jerusalem 5
Heydrich 17
Holocaust 1, 14, 87, 110–112
Holocaust Museum, Washington 8

Infectious Diseases Hospital 30, 74
Israel 77, 81, 100
Itzigsohn, Trude 96, 98

Jaeger, Karl 16, 18–19, 29, 39, 104–105, 112
Jewish Affairs specialists 17, 29–30

Jewish Hospital 5–6
Jordan, Fritz 29–30, 41–42
Jordan certificates (Jordanscheine) 30
Jost, Heinz 103–104
joys 78

Kadushin, George 8
Kalvarija 3, 89
Kant, Emmanuel 6
Kaplan, Elimelech 25
Kaunas 4, 17, 18, 20, 86
Kelzon, Shlomo 43
KGB 12
Koenigsberg 6
  University of 4
Koppelman, Michael 25, 27
Kovno 4
Krisciukacio Street 42

Landsberg-Dachau 96
Latvia 16, 88
Lavon, Pinchas 8
Lazdijai 9
Levin, Hirsch 11, 25, 27, 35
Libau, Latvia 8
Life certificates (Lebensscheine) 30
Lithuanian Republic 4
Littman, Sol 2, 32
Lloyd's of London 25
Lukas, Judge 103–104
Lurie, Esther 3, 8–9

Maccabi Sports Association 9
Majdanek 76, 83
Malbin, Esther 6
Malbin, Hans 97–98
Malbin, Moses 6
Marijampole 9
Maxwell, Dr. Elizabeth 110
Menschlichkeit 111
Miller (Ghetto ruler) 80
Mishell, William 25, 42, 78, 83
Moltke, Captain von 99

Nabriski, Dr. 104–105
New Year, Jewish 78
Ninth Fort 30, 32–39, 79, 89–90, 94

Oberjude 20, 22–23
Oder, River 4
Oleiski, Dr. Jacob 75
Orsha 4
Oshry, Rabbi Ephraim 2

Palciauskas, Kazys 20
Palestine 9
Paneriu Street 19
partisans 44, 76, 79, 84
Passover 78
Paukstys, Reverend Bronius 12, 76
Paulus, von 79
pogroms 27
Pohl, SS General 18
Police force 27, 37, 38, 73, 78–79, 85, 86
Porat, Professor Dina 2

Rabinovitch, Dr. Ephraim 17, 18, 25
Rauca, Helmut 16, 17, 28, 29, 32–35, 37
Red Army 9
Red Cross 91
Region Kaunas 17
registration cards 75
Reich, the 16
resistance 27
Riga 16
Romanovski, Basja 10
Romanovski, Benjamin 10
Rosenberg, Dr. Alfred 106
Rosh Hakahal 23
Rosh Hashanah 85
Rostovski, Leon 25
Russian Army 111
Russian occupation 10, 12
Russian Revolution 4

Schmitz, Heinrich 16, 17, 32
Schmukler, Rabbi 18, 23–24, 25
Schtitz, SS Sergeant 104–105
Schtrauch, Dr. 103
Schwabe, Dr. Moshe 5
Segal, Dr. Elie 44
Segalson, Moshe 44
segregation 17
selection 37, 89
Seventh Fort 16, 19, 27
Shapiro, Chief Rabbi Avraham Kahane 17, 35
Shapiro, Dr. Nachman 43, 75
Sheinson, Shulamith 11–12, 77
Sheinson (Tory), Pnina 11–12, 76, 78, 87
Shloshim 97
Siauliai 86, 89, 94
slave labor brigades 29, 40
Slobotka 16, 18
Slobotka Yeshiva 18
Smidt, Ben Zion 42
Snieg, Rabbi 18, 25
Sobibor 76
Soviet occupation 10
Stahlecker, Franz 16
Stalingrad 79, 83
Stutthof Concentration Camp 8, 96, 98, 102, 108
Sutzkever, Avraham 13
Symphony 78

Talmud 4
Tel Aviv University 14
Tornbaum, Captain 37
Tory, Avraham (Golub) 2, 9–14, 20, 25–26, 77, 83, 87, 103
Transfers Committee 20
Treblinka 83
typhus epidemic 74

Urals 4
Ushpitz, Pnina 11

Varshevski, Segal 44
Vassilenko, Captain 39
Viljampole (Slobotka) 18–19, 84, 88
Vilna 76, 84, 88
    forests 39, 83
Voschin, Dr. 104–105

Waffen SS 18
Wannsee conference 17
Warsaw Ghetto 76, 83
Weizmann Institute 13
White Russians 4
Wissen und Gewissen 34
Wolff, Dr. Grigory 21
Work 40–76
    elementary school 44
    kindergarten 44
    vegetable gardens 44
workshops 41, 43, 44, 79
work cards 30
World War I 4

Yarnton Trust Lecture 110
yellow star, order of 26, 81
Yom Kippur 78, 85–86

Zacharin, Dr. Benjamin 31, 74
Zilberg, Dr. Abrasha 102
Zionist underground 76
Zionist youth movement 9
Zussman Award 9